100

Best
Stir-Fries

100

Best
Stir-Fries

The ultimate guide to great stir-fries including

100 delicious recipes

First published in 2012
LOVE FOOD is an imprint of Parragon Books Ltd

Parragon
Queen Street House
4 Queen Street
Bath BA1 1HE, UK

www.parragon.com

ISBN: 978-1-4454-6193-9

Printed in Indonesia

Introduction by Linda Doeser
Cover photography by Clive Streeter

Notes for the Reader
This book uses both metric and imperial measurements. Follow the same
units of measurement throughout; do not mix metric and imperial. All
spoon measurements are level: teaspoons are assumed to be 5 ml, and
tablespoons are assumed to be 15 ml. Unless otherwise stated, milk is
assumed to be full fat, eggs and individual vegetables are medium, and
pepper is freshly ground black pepper.

The times given are an approximate guide only. Preparation times differ
according to the techniques used by different people and the cooking
times may also vary from those given. Optional ingredients, variations
or serving suggestions have not been included in the calculations.

Recipes using raw or very lightly cooked eggs should be avoided by
infants, the elderly, pregnant women, convalescents and anyone suffering
from an illness. Pregnant and breastfeeding women are advised to avoid
eating peanuts and peanut products, smoked or cured meats and fish
and unpasteurized dairy products. Sufferers from nut allergies should be
aware that some of the ready-made ingredients used in the recipes in this
book may contain nuts. Always check the packaging before use.

CONTENTS

INTRODUCTION

It might have been invented centuries ago in China, but stir-frying is the perfect technique for today's busy Western cook. A huge array of sensational dishes can be prepared and cooked quickly and easily, whether for midweek family suppers or informal entertaining.

The secret of stir-frying is very simple. Ingredients are finely chopped or thinly sliced so that they are all about the same size and then added to a hot pan, preferably a wok, containing a little oil. Aromatics, such as garlic and spring onions, are added first, then the ingredients that require longer cooking, such as meat and denser vegetables, and, finally, the quick-cooking items, such as green vegetables and noodles. The contents of the wok are stirred and tossed throughout the cooking time. This ensures that they are cooked through very rapidly without losing their colour, texture or nutrients.

It is possible to stir-fry in a frying pan but using a wok is far easier and more effective. This deep pan with sloping sides is designed for the continuous movement of the contents as they are tossed and return to the centre where the heat is most intense. The best woks are made of carbon steel or cast-iron; stainless steel tends to scorch. A round-based wok works well on a gas hob and one with a slightly flattened base is suitable for electric or ceramic hobs. A good size for a family is a wok with a diameter of 35 cm/14 inches as it allows plenty of room for stirring without being awkward to handle.

Top tips

• Only very tender cuts of meat and poultry and perfectly fresh vegetables are suitable for stir-frying because cooking takes such a short amount of time.

• Prepare all the ingredients before you start to cook and make sure you have any flavourings, such as soy sauce, to hand. There's no time for chopping or slicing once the first ingredients have gone into the wok.

• Use a sharp cook's knife or a Chinese cleaver for slicing and chopping. Slice denser vegetables, such as carrots and courgettes, diagonally. Exposing a large surface area to the heat ensures even and quick cooking.

• Always cut beef across the grain; lamb, pork and chicken may be cut across or along the grain.

• Preheat the empty wok over a high heat before adding the oil and swirling it to coat the base and halfway up the sides. You need far less oil than for ordinary pan-frying.

• Add the ingredients in the order specified in the recipe, and cook, stirring and tossing them from the centre to the sides of the wok.

Seasoning the wok

Manufacturers protect steel and cast-iron woks with a coating to prevent rust. Heat the new wok, scrub in warm soapy water to remove the coating, then rinse and dry. The manufacturer's instructions will describe how to season the wok, usually by repeatedly rubbing with vegetable oil, heating and then rubbing off the oil with kitchen paper. Once the wok has been seasoned, do not scrub again; simply wash in hot water.

1

STARTERS, SOUPS & SALADS

01

Spring Rolls

MAKES 20–25 PIECES

6 dried Chinese mushrooms, soaked in warm water for 20 minutes

1 tbsp vegetable or groundnut oil, plus extra for deep-frying

225 g/8 oz minced pork

1 tsp dark soy sauce

100 g/3 1/2 oz canned bamboo shoots, rinsed and julienned

100 g/3 1/2 oz raw prawns, peeled, deveined and chopped

225 g/8 oz beansprouts, trimmed and roughly chopped

1 tbsp spring onions, finely chopped

20–25 spring roll wrappers

1 egg white, lightly beaten

salt

Method

1 Squeeze out any excess water from the mushrooms and finely slice, discarding any tough stems.

2 In a preheated wok or deep pan, heat the oil and stir-fry the pork until it changes colour.

3 Add the dark soy sauce, bamboo shoots, mushrooms and a little salt to taste. Stir over a high heat for 3 minutes.

4 Add the prawns and cook for 2 minutes, then add the beansprouts and cook for a further minute. Remove from the heat and stir in the spring onions. Leave to cool.

5 Place a tablespoon of the mixture towards the bottom of a wrapper. Roll once to secure the filling, then fold in the sides to create a 10-cm/4-inch piece and continue to roll up. Seal with egg white.

6 Heat enough oil for deep-frying in a wok, deep-fat fryer or large heavy-based saucepan until it reaches 180–190°C/ 350–375°F, or until a cube of bread browns in 30 seconds. Fry the rolls for about 5 minutes, until golden brown and crispy.

7 Transfer the spring rolls to serving bowls and serve.

02

Crispy Pork Dumplings

SERVES 4

3 spring onions, roughly chopped

1 garlic clove, roughly chopped

1 small fresh red chilli, deseeded and
   roughly chopped

250 g/9 oz fresh pork mince

1 tsp salt

20 wonton wrappers

groundnut oil or vegetable oil,
   for deep-frying

chillies, cut into flowers, to garnish

Method

1 Put the spring onions, garlic, chilli, pork and salt in a food processor and process to a smooth paste.

2 Remove the wonton wrappers from the packet, but keep them in a pile and cover with a clean, damp tea towel to prevent them drying out. Lay one wrapper on a work surface in front of you in a diamond shape and brush the edges with water. Put a small amount of filling near one edge and fold the wrapper over the filling. Press the edges together to seal the parcel and shape into a semicircle like a pasty. Repeat with the remaining wrappers and filling.

3 Heat the oil in a wok, deep saucepan or deep-fat fryer to 180–190°C/350–375°F, or until a cube of bread browns in 30 seconds. Add the dumplings, in batches, and cook for 45 seconds–1 minute until crisp and golden all over. Remove with a slotted spoon, drain on kitchen paper and keep warm while you cook the remaining dumplings. Serve immediately, garnished with chilli flowers.

03

Pork & Cabbage Gyoza

MAKES 24 PIECES

24 gyoza wonton skins

2 tbsp water, for brushing

oil, for pan-frying

2 tbsp Japanese rice vinegar

2 tbsp shoyu (Japanese soy sauce)

Filling

*100 g/3½ oz Napa cabbage,
 finely shredded*

2 spring onions, finely chopped

115 g/4 oz fresh pork mince

*1-cm/½-inch piece fresh ginger,
 finely grated*

2 garlic cloves, crushed

1 tbsp shoyu (Japanese soy sauce)

2 tsp mirin

pinch of white pepper

salt, to taste

Method

1 To make the filling, mix all the ingredients together in a bowl.

2 Lay a gyoza wonton skin in the palm of your hand and place 1 heaped teaspoon of the filling in the centre. Brush a little water around the edges of the wonton skin.

3 Fold the skin sides up to meet in a ridge along the centre and press the edges together. Brush the curved edges of the skin with a little more water and make a series of little folds along the edges.

4 Repeat with the remaining gyoza wonton wrappers and filling. Heat a little oil in a wok or deep lidded frying pan and add as many gyoza as will fill the bottom of the pan with just a little space in between.

5 Cook for 2 minutes, or until browned. Add water to a depth of 3 mm/⅛ inch, cover the pan, and let simmer over a low heat for 6 minutes, or until the wrappers are translucent and cooked. Remove and keep warm while you cook the remaining gyoza.

6 Put the vinegar in a small dipping dish, stir in the shoyu, and add a splash of water.

7 Transfer the gyoza to a serving dish and serve with the sauce for dipping.

04

Chinese Rice with Egg

SERVES 2

2 tsp groundnut or vegetable oil

a few drops of sesame oil

1 small garlic clove, finely chopped

pinch of Chinese five-spice
    seasoning

1 carrot, diced

2 baby corn, halved and thinly sliced

2 tbsp water

small handful of baby spinach,
    coarse stalks removed,
    finely sliced

175 g/6 oz cooked brown or white
    rice, chilled

dash of soy sauce

1 tsp sesame seeds (optional)

small knob of butter

1 egg, beaten

Method

1 Heat a wok over a medium–high heat, then add the oils. Add the garlic, five-spice seasoning, carrot and baby corn and stir-fry for 5 minutes, stirring and tossing constantly to prevent the spices and vegetables from burning and sticking.

2 Add the water and stir-fry for 2 minutes, then mix in the spinach and cook, stirring frequently, for a further 2 minutes, or until the vegetables are tender.

3 Add the rice and soy sauce to the wok and heat through. Mix in the sesame seeds, if using.

4 Meanwhile, melt the butter in a small heavy-based frying pan and add the egg. Swirl the egg until it covers the base of the pan. Cook until the egg has set and is cooked through, then turn out onto a plate. Cut the omelette into strips or pieces.

5 Transfer the rice to individual serving bowls and arrange the omelette on top.

05

Prawn Toasts

MAKES 16 PIECES

100 g/3 1/2 oz raw prawns,
   peeled and deveined

2 egg whites

2 tbsp cornflour

1/2 tsp sugar

pinch of salt

2 tbsp finely chopped fresh
   coriander leaves

2 slices day-old white bread

vegetable or groundnut oil,
   for deep-frying

Method

1 Pound the prawns to a pulp with a pestle in a mortar.

2 Mix the prawns with one of the egg whites and
1 tablespoon of the cornflour. Add the sugar and salt and
stir in the coriander. Mix the remaining egg white with the
remaining cornflour.

3 Remove the crusts from the bread and cut each slice into
8 triangles. Brush the top of each piece with the egg white and
cornflour mixture, then add 1 teaspoon of the prawn mixture.
Smooth the top.

4 Heat enough oil for deep-frying in a wok, deep-fat fryer or
large heavy-based saucepan until it reaches 180–190°C/
350–375°F, or until a cube of bread browns in 30 seconds. Fry
the toasts prawn-side down for about 2 minutes. Turn and fry
for a further 2 minutes until golden.

5 Remove the prawn toasts with a slotted spoon, drain on
kitchen paper and serve warm.

06

Crispy Sesame Prawns

SERVES 4

115 g/4 oz self-raising flour

3 tbsp sesame seeds, toasted or
  dry-fried

1 tsp Thai red curry paste

1 tbsp Thai fish sauce

150 ml/5 fl oz water

vegetable or groundnut oil,
  for deep-frying

20 large, uncooked prawns, peeled
  and deveined with tails intact

chilli sauce, to serve

Method

1 Combine the flour and sesame seeds in a bowl. Stir together
the curry paste, fish sauce and water in a jug until mixed. Gradually
pour the liquid into the flour, stirring constantly, to make a
thick batter.

2 Heat a large wok over a high heat. Pour in the oil and heat to
180–190°C/350–375°F or until a cube of bread browns in
30 seconds. Holding the prawns by their tails, dip them into the
batter, one at a time, then carefully drop into the hot oil. Cook for
2–3 minutes, until crisp and brown. Drain on kitchen paper.

3 Serve immediately with chilli sauce.

07

Crab Wontons

SERVES 4

1 tbsp groundnut or vegetable oil,
  plus extra for deep-frying

2.5-cm/1-inch piece fresh ginger,
  peeled and finely chopped

1/4 red pepper, deseeded and
  finely chopped

handful of fresh coriander, chopped

1/4 tsp salt

150 g/5 1/2 oz canned white
  crabmeat, drained

20 wonton wrappers

water, for brushing

sweet chilli dipping sauce, to serve

Method

1 Heat the oil in a preheated wok.

2 Add the ginger and red pepper and stir-fry over a high heat for 30 seconds.

3 Add the coriander and mix well. Leave to cool, then add the salt and the crabmeat and mix well. Meanwhile remove the wonton wrappers from the packet, but keep them in a pile and cover with a clean, damp tea towel to prevent them drying out.

4 Lay one wrapper on a work surface in front of you and brush the edges with water. Put a teaspoonful of the crabmeat mixture in the centre and fold the wrapper over the mixture to form a triangle.

5 Press the edges together to seal. Fold each side corner up to the top corner to make a small parcel, brushing the edges with water to seal if necessary. Repeat with the remaining wrappers and crabmeat mixture.

6 Heat the oil for deep-frying in the wok or a deep saucepan or deep-fat fryer to 180–190°C/350–375°F, or until a cube of bread browns in 30 seconds.

7 Add the wontons, in batches, and cook for 45 seconds– 1 minute until crisp and golden all over.

8 Remove with a slotted spoon, drain on kitchen paper and keep warm while you cook the remaining wontons.

9 Serve with sweet chilli dipping sauce.

08

Tempura Vegetables

SERVES 4

150 g/5½ oz packet tempura mix

4 shiitake mushrooms

4 fresh asparagus spears

4 slices sweet potato

1 red pepper, deseeded and
  cut into strips

4 onion slices, cut into rings

oil, for deep-frying

Dipping sauce

2 tsp mirin

1 tbsp shoyu (Japanese soy sauce)

pinch of dashi granules, dissolved in
  2 tbsp boiling water

Method

1 To make the dipping sauce, mix the ingredients together in a small dipping dish.

2 Mix the tempura with water according to the packet instructions.

3 Drop the vegetables into the batter.

4 Heat enough oil for deep-frying in a wok, deep-fat fryer or large heavy-based saucepan until it reaches 180–190°C/350–375°F, or until a cube of bread browns in 30 seconds.

5 Lift 2–3 pieces of the vegetables out of the batter, add to the oil, and cook for 2–3 minutes, or until the batter is a light golden colour.

6 Remove the tempura vegetables with a slotted spoon and drain on kitchen paper. Keep hot while you cook the remaining pieces. Transfer the tempura vegetables to a serving dish and serve with the dipping sauce.

09

Crispy 'Seaweed'

SERVES 4

*250 g/9 oz dark green
  cabbage leaves*

groundnut oil, for deep-frying

1 tsp caster sugar

1/2 tsp salt

4 tbsp flaked almonds, to garnish

Method

1 Remove and discard the tough stalks from the cabbage leaves. Wash the leaves, drain thoroughly and spread out on kitchen paper to dry.

2 Stack a few leaves and roll up tightly. Using a very sharp knife, slice crossways into the thinnest possible shreds. Repeat with the remaining leaves. Spread out the shreds on kitchen paper and leave until completely dry.

3 Heat a large wok over a high heat. Pour in the oil and heat to 180°C/350°F or until a cube of bread browns in 30 seconds. Remove the wok from the heat and add half the shredded leaves. Return the wok to the heat and deep-fry until the shreds begin to float to the surface and become crisp. Remove with a slotted spoon and drain on kitchen paper. Keep warm while you deep-fry the rest.

4 Tip the shreds into a warm serving bowl. Combine the sugar and salt, and sprinkle over the 'seaweed', tossing to mix.

5 Quickly fry the flaked almonds in the hot oil. Remove with a slotted spoon and sprinkle over the 'seaweed'. Serve warm or at room temperature.

10

Beef & Noodle Soup

SERVES 4

4 shallots, chopped

1 large garlic clove, chopped

2 tsp finely chopped fresh ginger

1 tbsp groundnut oil

450 g/1 lb sirloin steak, external
    fat removed, cut into
    1-cm/1/2-inch cubes

1.3 litres/2 1/4 pints beef stock

1 tsp white peppercorns, crushed

150 g/5 1/2 oz flat rice noodles

juice of 1 lime

2 tsp Thai fish sauce

1/2 tsp salt

1/2 tsp sugar

To garnish

4 spring onions, shredded

slivers of red chilli

3 tbsp torn coriander leaves

3 tbsp torn basil leaves

lime wedges

Method

1 Purée the shallots, garlic and ginger in a food processor or blender, pulsing several times until the purée is fairly smooth.

2 Heat a wok over a medium–high heat, then add the oil and stir-fry the paste for 2 minutes, taking care not to let it burn. Add the beef and stir-fry for 1 minute until brown, then pour in 1 litre/1 3/4 pints of the stock. Bring to a rolling boil, skimming off any foam that forms. Add the crushed peppercorns, then reduce the heat and gently simmer for 30–35 minutes, or until the meat is tender.

3 Meanwhile, soak the noodles in enough lukewarm water to cover for 15 minutes, or cook according to the instructions on the packet, until soft.

4 When the meat is tender, stir in any sticky residue that has formed at the edge of the wok. Add the remaining stock, the lime juice, fish sauce, salt and sugar. Simmer for a few minutes.

5 Drain the noodles and divide between individual soup bowls. Ladle the meat and broth over the top. Serve with the garnishes sprinkled over the soup.

11

Sweet & Sour Spare Ribs

SERVES 4

450 g/1 lb spare ribs, cut into
  bite-sized pieces

1½ tbsp vegetable or groundnut oil,
  plus extra for deep-frying

1 green pepper, deseeded and
  roughly chopped

1 small onion, roughly chopped

1 small carrot, finely sliced

½ tsp finely chopped garlic

½ tsp finely chopped fresh ginger

100 g/3½ oz pineapple chunks

Marinade

2 tsp light soy sauce

½ tsp salt

pinch of white pepper

Sauce

3 tbsp white rice vinegar

2 tbsp sugar

1 tbsp light soy sauce

1 tbsp tomato ketchup

Method

1 Combine all the marinade ingredients in a bowl. Add the spare ribs and leave to marinate for at least 20 minutes.

2 Heat a large wok over a high heat. Pour in the oil and heat to 180°C/350°F or until a cube of bread browns in 30 seconds.

3 Deep-fry the spare ribs for 8 minutes. Drain and set aside.

4 To prepare the sauce, mix together the vinegar, sugar, light soy sauce and ketchup. Set aside.

5 In the preheated wok, heat 1 tablespoon of the oil and stir-fry the pepper, onion and carrot for 2 minutes. Remove and set aside. Wipe the wok clean.

6 In a clean preheated wok, heat ½ tablespoon of oil and stir-fry the garlic and ginger until fragrant. Add the sauce. Bring back to the boil and add the pineapple chunks. Finally add the spare ribs and the pepper, onion and carrot. Stir until warmed through and serve immediately.

12

Chicken Noodle Soup

SERVES 4–6

250 g/9 oz medium egg noodles

1 tbsp corn oil

4 skinless, boneless chicken thighs,
    diced

1 bunch of spring onions, sliced,
    white and green kept separate

2 garlic cloves, chopped

2-cm/3/4-inch piece fresh ginger,
    finely chopped

850 ml/1 1/2 pints chicken stock

175 ml/6 fl oz coconut milk

3 tsp Thai red curry paste

3 tbsp peanut butter

2 tbsp light soy sauce

1 small red pepper, deseeded and
    chopped

55 g/2 oz frozen peas

salt and pepper

Method

1 Cook the noodles in a saucepan of boiling water for 4 minutes,
or according to the instructions on the packet, until soft.

2 Heat a wok over a medium–high heat, then add the oil. Add the
chicken and stir-fry for 5 minutes, or until lightly browned. Add the
white part of the spring onions, the garlic and ginger and
stir-fry for 2 minutes.

3 Add the stock, coconut milk, curry paste, peanut butter and
soy sauce. Season to taste with salt and pepper. Bring to the boil,
stirring constantly, then simmer for 8 minutes, stirring occasionally.
Add the pepper, peas and green spring onion tops and cook for a
further 2 minutes.

4 Drain the noodles, then add them to the wok and heat through.
Spoon into soup bowls and serve immediately.

13

Squid & Prawn Laksa

SERVES 4

225 g/8 oz dried wide rice noodles

700 ml/1¼ pints canned coconut milk

2 fish stock cubes

3 fresh kaffir lime leaves

2 tbsp Thai red curry paste

bunch of spring onions, roughly chopped

2 fresh red chillies, deseeded and roughly chopped

225 g/8 oz raw squid, cleaned and cut into rings

225 g/8 oz large raw prawns, peeled and deveined

handful of fresh coriander, chopped, plus extra leaves to garnish

Method

1 Soak the noodles in a saucepan of boiling water for 4 minutes, covered, or cook according to the packet instructions, until tender. Drain, rinse under cold running water and set aside.

2 Put the coconut milk, stock cubes, lime leaves, curry paste, spring onions and chillies in a wok, and bring gently to the boil, stirring occasionally. Reduce the heat and simmer, stirring occasionally, for 2–3 minutes, until the stock cubes and paste have dissolved.

3 Add the squid and prawns and simmer for 1–2 minutes, until the squid has plumped up and the prawns have turned pink. Add the cooked noodles and the chopped coriander and stir well. Ladle into individual bowls and serve immediately, garnished with coriander leaves.

14

Hot & Sour Soup Tom Yum

SERVES 4

2 fresh red chillies, deseeded
and roughly chopped

6 tbsp rice vinegar

1.2 litres/2 pints vegetable stock

2 lemon grass stalks, halved

4 tbsp soy sauce

1 tbsp palm sugar

juice of ½ lime

2 tbsp groundnut or vegetable oil

225 g/8 oz firm tofu
(drained weight), cut into
1-cm/½-inch cubes

400 g/14 oz canned straw
mushrooms, drained

4 spring onions, chopped

1 small head pak choi, shredded

Method

1 Mix the chillies and vinegar together in a non-metallic bowl, cover and leave to stand at room temperature for 1 hour.

2 Meanwhile, bring the stock to the boil in a saucepan. Add the lemon grass, soy sauce, sugar and lime juice, reduce the heat and simmer for 20–30 minutes.

3 Heat the oil in a preheated wok, add the tofu cubes and stir-fry over a high heat for 2–3 minutes, or until browned all over. (You may need to do this in 2 batches, depending on the size of the wok.)

4 Remove with a slotted spoon and drain on kitchen paper.

5 Add the chillies and vinegar with the tofu, mushrooms and half the spring onions to the stock mixture and cook for 10 minutes.

6 Mix the remaining spring onions with the pak choi.

7 Scatter over the spring onions and pak choi and serve.

15

Thai-style Seafood Soup

SERVES 4

1.3 litres/2¼ pints fish stock

1 lemon grass stalk, split lengthways

*pared rind of ½ lime or
1 fresh kaffir lime leaf*

*2.5-cm/1-inch piece fresh ginger,
sliced*

¼ tsp chilli paste, or to taste

4–6 spring onions

*200 g/7 oz large or medium raw
prawns, peeled and deveined*

250 g/9 oz scallops (16–20)

2 tbsp coriander leaves

salt

fresh red chilli rings, to garnish

Method

1 Pour the stock into a wok with the lemon grass, lime rind, ginger and chilli paste. Bring just to the boil, then reduce the heat and simmer, covered, for 10–15 minutes.

2 Cut the spring onions in half lengthways, then slice crossways very thinly. Cut the prawns almost in half lengthways, keeping the tails intact.

3 Pour the stock through a sieve, then return to the wok and bring to a simmer, with bubbles rising at the edges and the surface trembling. Add the spring onions and cook for 2–3 minutes. Taste and season with salt, if needed. Stir in a little more chilli paste if wished.

4 Add the scallops and prawns and poach for 1 minute, or until the scallops turn opaque and the prawns curl.

5 Drop in the coriander leaves, then ladle the soup into bowls, dividing the shellfish evenly, and garnish with chilli rings.

16

Mushroom & Ginger Soup

SERVES 4

15 g/1/2 oz dried Chinese mushrooms

1 litre/13/4 pints hot vegetable stock

125 g/41/2 oz thread egg noodles

2 tsp sunflower oil

3 garlic cloves, crushed

2.5-cm/1-inch piece fresh ginger, finely shredded

1/2 tsp mushroom ketchup

1 tsp light soy sauce

125 g/41/2 oz beansprouts

fresh coriander sprigs, to garnish

Method

1 Soak the dried Chinese mushrooms for at least 30 minutes in 300 ml/10 fl oz of the hot stock. Drain the mushrooms and reserve the stock. Remove the stalks of the mushrooms and discard. Slice the caps and reserve.

2 Cook the noodles according to the instructions on the packet. Drain well, rinse under cold water, and drain again. Set aside.

3 Heat the oil in a preheated wok or large frying pan over a high heat. Add the garlic and ginger, stir and add the mushrooms. Stir over a high heat for 2 minutes.

4 Add the remaining stock to the reserved stock and bring to the boil. Add the mushroom ketchup and soy sauce. Stir in the beansprouts and cook until tender.

5 Place some noodles in each soup bowl and ladle the soup on top. Garnish with fresh coriander sprigs and serve immediately.

17

Rainbow Salad

SERVES 3–4

6 large shiitake mushrooms

10 spring onions, green part included

6 carrots

3 tbsp rapeseed oil

1 red pepper, deseeded and finely sliced

8 baby corn, halved diagonally

250 g/9 oz fresh beansprouts

salt

a few small mint leaves, to garnish

4 tbsp toasted coconut ribbons, to garnish

Dressing

1/2–1 green chilli, deseeded and very finely chopped

1 tsp sugar

1 1/2 tbsp lime juice

2 tsp Thai fish sauce

2 tbsp chopped mint

2 tbsp rapeseed oil

6 tbsp coconut cream

salt

Method

1 First make the dressing. Using a mortar and pestle, pound the chopped chilli and the sugar to a watery green paste. Add the lime juice, fish sauce and a pinch of salt, stirring to dissolve the sugar. Pour into a blender with the mint, oil and coconut cream. Purée until smooth and set aside.

2 Remove and discard the tough stalks from the mushrooms, and thinly slice the caps. Halve the spring onions lengthways, then slice into 2.5-cm/1-inch lengths, keeping the green and white parts separate.

3 Using a swivel peeler, shave the carrots into thin slivers. Heat a wok over a high heat, then add 3 tablespoons of the oil. Stir-fry the mushrooms, red pepper, baby corn and the white spring onions for 2 minutes. Add the carrots, beansprouts, green spring onions and salt to taste. Toss for 1 minute until the vegetables are only just cooked and still crunchy.

4 Transfer to a colander set over a bowl to cool. Discard any drained liquid and tip into a serving bowl. Toss with the dressing, then sprinkle with mint leaves and the toasted coconut ribbons. Serve at room temperature.

18

Chinese Chicken Salad

SERVES 4

3 boneless, skinless chicken breasts,
   weighing 450 g/1 lb in total,
   cut into bite-sized pieces

2 tsp soy sauce

1/4 tsp freshly ground white pepper

2 tbsp groundnut oil, plus extra for
   deep-frying

50 g/1¾ oz thin rice noodles

1/2 head Chinese leaves,
   thinly sliced diagonally

3 spring onions, green parts included,
   sliced diagonally

40 g/1½ oz almonds with skin,
   sliced lengthways

2 tsp sesame seeds, to garnish

Dressing

5 tbsp olive oil

3 tbsp rice vinegar

3 tbsp light soy sauce

a few drops sesame oil

salt and pepper

Method

1 Sprinkle the chicken with the soy sauce and white pepper.
Combine the dressing ingredients and whisk to blend.

2 Heat a wok over a high heat, then add the groundnut oil.
Stir-fry the chicken for 4–5 minutes until brown and crisp.
Drain on kitchen paper and allow to cool. Wipe out the wok.

3 Pour enough groundnut oil for deep-frying into the wok.
Heat to 180°C/350°F or until a cube of bread browns in
30 seconds, then fry a few noodles at a time until puffed up
and crisp. Drain on kitchen paper.

4 Arrange the Chinese leaves in a shallow serving dish. Place
the noodles in a pile on top of the leaves on one side of the
dish. Arrange the chicken, spring onion and almonds in the
remaining space. Whisk the dressing again and pour over the
salad. Garnish with the sesame seeds and serve.

19

Gingered Chicken Salad

SERVES 4

4 skinless, boneless chicken breasts

4 spring onions, chopped

2.5-cm/1-inch piece fresh ginger, finely chopped

2 garlic cloves, crushed

2 tbsp vegetable or groundnut oil

Salad

1 tbsp vegetable or groundnut oil

1 onion, sliced

2 garlic cloves, chopped

115 g/4 oz baby sweetcorn, halved

115 g/4 oz mangetout, halved lengthways

1 red pepper, deseeded and sliced

7.5-cm/3-inch piece cucumber, peeled, deseeded and sliced

4 tbsp Thai soy sauce

1 tbsp jaggery or soft light brown sugar

a few Thai basil leaves

175 g/6 oz fine egg noodles

Method

1 Cut the chicken into 2.5-cm/1-inch cubes. Mix the spring onions, ginger, garlic and oil together in a shallow dish and add the chicken. Cover and marinate for at least 3 hours. Lift the meat out of the marinade and set aside.

2 Heat the oil in a wok, add the onion and cook for 1–2 minutes. Add the garlic and the rest of the vegetables, except the cucumber, and cook for 2–3 minutes until just tender. Add the cucumber, half the soy sauce, the sugar and the basil, and mix gently.

3 Soak the noodles for 2–3 minutes (check the packet instructions), or until tender, and drain well. Sprinkle the remaining soy sauce over them and arrange on plates. Top with the cooked vegetables.

4 Add a little more oil to the wok if necessary, add the chicken and cook over a fairly high heat until browned on all sides. Arrange the chicken on top of the salad and serve hot or warm.

20

Hot & Sour Vegetable Salad

SERVES 4

2 tbsp vegetable or groundnut oil

1 tbsp chilli oil

1 onion, sliced

2.5-cm/1-inch piece fresh ginger, grated

1 small head of broccoli, cut into florets

2 carrots, cut into short thin sticks

1 red pepper, deseeded and cut into squares

1 yellow pepper, deseeded and cut into strips

55 g/2 oz mangetout

55 g/2 oz baby corn, halved

Dressing

2 tbsp vegetable or groundnut oil

1 tsp chilli oil

1 tbsp rice wine vinegar

juice of 1 lime

1/2 tsp Thai fish sauce

Method

1 Heat a wok over a medium–high heat and add the oils. Sauté the onion and ginger for 1–2 minutes until they start to soften. Add the vegetables and stir-fry for 2–3 minutes until they have softened slightly. Remove from the heat and set aside.

2 Mix together the dressing ingredients. Transfer the vegetables to a serving plate and drizzle the dressing over. Serve warm immediately, or let the flavours develop and serve cold.

21

Spicy Warm Crab & Prawn Salad

SERVES 4

1 tbsp groundnut or vegetable oil

1 fresh serrano chilli, deseeded and
  finely chopped

115 g/4 oz mangetout, cut in half
  diagonally

6 spring onions, finely shredded

25 g/1 oz frozen sweetcorn kernels,
  thawed

150 g/5½ oz white crabmeat,
  drained if canned

55 g/2 oz raw prawns, peeled and
  deveined

1 carrot, grated

115 g/4 oz fresh beansprouts

225 g/8 oz baby spinach leaves,
  coarse stalks removed

1 tbsp finely grated orange rind

2 tbsp orange juice

1 tbsp chopped fresh coriander,
  to garnish

Method

1 Heat a wok over a medium heat, then add the oil. Add the chilli
and mangetout, then stir-fry for 2 minutes.

2 Add the spring onions and sweetcorn and continue to stir-fry for
a further minute.

3 Add the crabmeat, prawns, carrot, beansprouts and spinach. Stir
in the orange rind and juice and stir-fry for 2–3 minutes, or until
the spinach has begun to wilt and everything is cooked.

4 Divide among four individual serving bowls, sprinkle with the
coriander and serve immediately.

22

Gado Gado

SERVES 4

3 tbsp groundnut oil

2 shallots, finely chopped

2 garlic cloves, crushed

1 red chilli, finely chopped

juice of 2 limes

225 g/8 oz crunchy peanut butter

250 ml/9 fl oz coconut milk

200 g/7 oz French beans

1/2 cucumber

1 red pepper

250 g/9 oz tempeh or firm tofu,
    diced

200 g/7 oz beansprouts

2 heads Little Gem lettuce, chopped

2 hard-boiled eggs, quartered

chopped coriander, to garnish

Method

1 Heat a wok over a medium heat and add 1 tablespoon of the oil. Fry the shallots and garlic for 2–3 minutes to soften but not brown.

2 Stir in the chilli, lime juice, peanut butter and coconut milk and stir over a medium heat for 2–3 minutes. Remove from the wok and cool.

3 Cut the beans into bite-sized pieces then blanch in boiling water for 2 minutes. Drain and rinse in cold water.

4 Halve the cucumber lengthways and slice diagonally. Deseed and thinly slice the red pepper.

5 Heat the remaining oil in the wok and fry the tempeh until golden on all sides. Drain on absorbent kitchen paper.

6 Toss together the beans, cucumber, red pepper, beansprouts and lettuce and arrange on a large platter.

7 Arrange the fried tempeh and hard-boiled eggs over the salad.

8 Spoon the dressing onto the salad and sprinkle with chopped coriander. Serve immediately.

2

MEAT

23

Sliced Beef in Black Bean Sauce

SERVES 4

3 tbsp groundnut oil

450 g/1 lb beef sirloin, thinly sliced

1 red pepper, deseeded and
   thinly sliced

1 green pepper, deseeded and
   thinly sliced

1 bunch spring onions, sliced

2 garlic cloves, crushed

1 tbsp grated fresh ginger

2 tbsp black bean sauce

1 tbsp sherry

1 tbsp soy sauce

Method

1 Heat 2 tablespoons of the oil in a wok and stir-fry the beef on a high heat for 1–2 minutes. Remove and set aside.

2 Add the remaining oil and peppers and stir-fry for 2 minutes. Remove and set aside.

3 Add the spring onions, garlic and ginger and stir-fry for 30 seconds.

4 Add the black bean sauce, sherry and soy sauce, then stir in the beef and heat until bubbling.

5 Transfer to bowls and serve.

24

Beef Chow Mein

SERVES 4

*280 g/10 oz fillet steak,
    cut into slivers*

225 g/8 oz dried egg noodles

2 tbsp vegetable or groundnut oil

1 onion, finely sliced

*1 green pepper, deseeded and
    finely sliced*

*140 g/5 oz fresh beansprouts,
    trimmed*

1 tsp salt

pinch of sugar

2 tsp Chinese rice wine

2 tbsp light soy sauce

1 tbsp dark soy sauce

1 tbsp finely shredded spring onion

Marinade

1 tsp light soy sauce

dash of sesame oil

1/2 tsp Chinese rice wine

pinch of white pepper

Method

1 Combine all the marinade ingredients in a bowl and marinate the beef for at least 20 minutes.

2 Cook the noodles according to the instructions on the packet. When cooked, rinse under cold water and set aside.

3 In a preheated wok or deep pan, heat the oil and stir-fry the beef for about 1 minute, until the meat has changed colour, then add the onion and cook for 1 minute, followed by the pepper and beansprouts. Evaporate off any water from the vegetables. Add the salt, sugar, rice wine and soy sauces. Stir in the noodles and toss for 1 minute. Finally, stir in the spring onion and serve.

25

Sichuan Peppered Beef

SERVES 4

2.5-cm/1-inch piece fresh ginger,
   grated

1 garlic clove, crushed

1 tbsp rice wine

1 tbsp soy sauce

1 tbsp hoisin sauce

2 tsp Sichuan peppercorns,
   without seeds, crushed

600 g/1 lb 5 oz beef fillet

3 tbsp groundnut oil

1 onion, thinly sliced

1 green pepper, deseeded and
   thinly sliced

Method

1 Mix together the ginger, garlic, rice wine, soy sauce, hoisin sauce and peppercorns in a wide, non-metallic bowl.

2 Thinly slice the beef into medallions and add to the bowl, turning to coat in the marinade. Cover and leave to marinate for 30 minutes.

3 Heat the oil in a wok and stir-fry the beef for 1–2 minutes to brown. Remove and keep to one side.

4 Add the onion and green pepper and stir-fry for 2 minutes. Add the beef with any marinade juices and stir to heat evenly.

5 Serve the beef immediately.

26

Beef Chop Suey

SERVES 4

450 g/1 lb ribeye steak, sliced

1 head of broccoli, cut into florets

2 tbsp vegetable oil

1 onion, sliced

2 sticks celery, sliced

225 g/8 oz mangetout,
  sliced lengthways

55 g/2 oz canned bamboo shoots,
  rinsed and shredded

8 water chestnuts, sliced

225 g/8 oz mushrooms, sliced

1 tbsp oyster sauce

1 tsp salt

Marinade

1 tbsp Shaoxing rice wine

1/2 tsp white pepper

1/2 tsp salt

1 tbsp light soy sauce

1/2 tsp sesame oil

Method

1 Combine all the marinade ingredients in a bowl and marinate the beef for at least 20 minutes.

2 Blanch the broccoli in a large pan of boiling water for 30 seconds. Drain and set aside.

3 In a preheated wok, heat 1 tablespoon of the oil and stir-fry the beef until the colour has changed. Remove and set aside.

4 Clean the wok, heat the remaining oil and stir-fry the onion for 1 minute. Add the celery and broccoli and cook for 2 minutes. Add the mangetout, bamboo shoots, water chestnuts and mushrooms and cook for 1 minute. Add the beef and season with the oyster sauce and salt.

5 Transfer to bowls and serve.

27

Hot Sesame Beef

SERVES 4

500 g/1 lb 2 oz beef fillet,
    cut into thin strips

1 1/2 tbsp sesame seeds

125 ml/4 fl oz beef stock

2 tbsp soy sauce

2 tbsp grated fresh ginger

2 garlic cloves, finely chopped

1 tsp cornflour

1/2 tsp chilli flakes

3 tbsp sesame oil

1 large head of broccoli,
    cut into florets

1 yellow pepper, deseeded and,
    thinly sliced

1 red chilli, deseeded and finely
    sliced

1 tbsp chilli oil, to taste

cooked wild rice, to serve

1 tbsp chopped fresh coriander,
    to garnish

Method

1 Mix the beef strips with 1 tablespoon of the sesame seeds in a small bowl. In a separate bowl, whisk together the beef stock, soy sauce, ginger, garlic, cornflour and chilli flakes.

2 Heat 1 tablespoon of the sesame oil in a large wok or frying pan. Stir-fry the beef strips for 2–3 minutes. Remove and set aside.

3 Discard any remaining oil in the pan, then wipe with kitchen paper to remove any stray sesame seeds. Heat the remaining oil, add the broccoli, pepper, chilli and chilli oil and stir-fry for 2–3 minutes. Stir in the beef stock mixture, cover and simmer for 2 minutes.

4 Return the beef to the wok and simmer until the juices thicken, stirring occasionally. Cook for another 1–2 minutes.

5 Sprinkle with the remaining sesame seeds. Serve over freshly cooked wild rice and garnish with fresh coriander.

28

Marinated Beef with Vegetables

SERVES 4

*500 g/1 lb 2 oz rump steak,
    cut into thin strips*

3 tbsp sesame oil

1/2 tbsp cornflour

1/2 tbsp soy sauce

1 head of broccoli, cut into florets

2 carrots, cut into thin strips

125 g/4 1/2 oz mangetout

125 ml/4 fl oz beef stock

250 g/9 oz baby spinach, shredded

*freshly cooked plain rice or noodles,
    to serve*

Marinade

1 tbsp dry sherry

1/2 tbsp soy sauce

1/2 tbsp cornflour

1/2 tsp caster sugar

2 garlic cloves, finely chopped

1 tbsp sesame oil

Method

1 To make the marinade, mix the sherry, soy sauce, cornflour, sugar, garlic and oil in a bowl. Add the beef to the mixture and cover with clingfilm. Set aside to marinate for 30 minutes, then remove the beef and discard the marinade.

2 Heat a wok over a medium–high heat, then add 1 tablespoon of the oil. Stir-fry the beef for 2 minutes, until medium–rare. Remove from the wok and set aside.

3 Combine the cornflour and soy sauce in a bowl and set aside. Pour the remaining 2 tablespoons of oil into the wok, add the broccoli, carrots and mangetout and stir-fry for 2 minutes.

4 Add the stock, cover the wok and cook for 1 minute. Stir in the spinach, beef and the cornflour mixture. Cook until the juices boil and thicken. Serve with cooked rice or noodles.

29

Ginger Beef with Yellow Peppers

SERVES 4

500 g/1 lb 2 oz beef fillet,
	cut into 2.5-cm/1-inch cubes

2 tsp groundnut oil

2 garlic cloves, crushed

2 tbsp grated fresh ginger

pinch of chilli flakes

2 yellow peppers, deseeded and
	thinly sliced

125 g/4½ oz baby corn

175 g/6 oz mangetout

freshly cooked rice noodles drizzled
	with sesame oil, to serve

Marinade

2 tbsp soy sauce

2 tsp groundnut oil

1½ tsp caster sugar

1 tsp cornflour

Method

1 To make the marinade, mix the soy sauce, oil, sugar and cornflour in a bowl. Stir in the beef, then cover with clingfilm and set aside to marinate for 30 minutes.

2 Heat a wok over a medium–high heat, then add the oil. Add the garlic, ginger and chilli flakes and cook for 30 seconds. Stir in the yellow peppers and baby corn, and stir-fry for 2 minutes. Add the mangetout and cook for a further minute.

3 Remove the vegetables from the wok. Add the beef and marinade to the wok and stir-fry for 3–4 minutes, or until cooked to taste. Return the vegetables to the wok, mix well and cook until all the ingredients are heated through. Remove from the heat and serve with cooked noodles.

30

Beef & Pak Choi Stir-fry

SERVES 4

350 g/12 oz skirt steak

2 tbsp groundnut oil

1 shallot, chopped

2 tsp finely chopped fresh ginger

1 fresh red chilli, deseeded and
thinly sliced

350 g/12 oz pak choi, stalks cut into
2.5-cm/1-inch squares and leaves
sliced into wide ribbons

1 tbsp cornflour

2 tbsp beef stock or water

3 tbsp chopped fresh coriander,
to garnish

Marinade

2 tbsp soy sauce

1 1/2 tbsp Chinese rice wine
or dry sherry

1/2 tsp sugar

1/2 tsp pepper

1/4 tsp salt

Method

1 Pound the steak with the blunt side of a knife. Slice diagonally across the grain into thin bite-sized pieces and put in a shallow bowl.

2 Combine the marinade ingredients in a bowl and pour over the beef, stirring to coat. Leave to marinate for 1 hour at room temperature, or overnight in the refrigerator.

3 Heat a wok over a medium–high heat, then add the oil. Stir-fry the shallot, ginger and chilli for 1 minute. Increase the heat to high and add the beef and marinade. Stir-fry for 3 minutes. Add the pak choi stalks and stir-fry for 1 minute. Add the leaves and stir-fry for a further minute.

4 Mix the cornflour and stock to a smooth paste. Add to the wok and stir-fry for 1 minute, until slightly thickened. Transfer to a warmed serving dish and garnish with the coriander. Serve immediately.

31

Beef with Mixed Mushrooms

SERVES 2–3

1½ tbsp Szechuan peppers

½ tsp salt

350 g/12 oz sirloin or rump steak

200 g/7 oz mixed small mushrooms, such as cremini, enoki and buna shimeji

½ tbsp cornflour

125 ml/4 fl oz beef stock

2 tsp Chinese rice wine or dry sherry

4 tsp soy sauce

3 tbsp groundnut or vegetable oil

1 shallot, finely chopped

1 tsp finely chopped fresh ginger

1 large garlic clove, thinly sliced

3 tbsp chopped fresh coriander, to garnish

Method

1 Place the Szechuan peppers in a mortar with the salt and grind with a pestle. Sprinkle over both sides of the meat, pressing in well. Slice the meat diagonally across the grain into thin bite-sized pieces and set aside.

2 Wipe the mushrooms with damp kitchen paper. If using clumping mushrooms, such as enoki and buna shimeji, cut off the root and separate the clump. Cut any large mushrooms in half.

3 Mix the cornflour to a paste with 2 tablespoons of the stock. Add the rice wine and soy sauce, mixing well.

4 Heat a wok over a medium–high heat, then add 1 tablespoon of the oil. Fry the shallot and ginger for 1 minute. Add the garlic and fry for a few seconds, then add the mushrooms and 2 tablespoons of the stock. Stir-fry for 4 minutes. Add the cornflour mixture and the remaining stock. Bring to the boil, stirring, then reduce the heat and simmer for 2 minutes. Transfer to a warmed serving dish.

5 Wipe out the wok with kitchen paper, then heat over a high heat. Add the remaining oil. Add the beef and stir-fry for 3 minutes. Add to the mushroom mixture and garnish with the coriander. Serve immediately.

32

Marinated Beef with Celery

SERVES 4

500 g/1 lb 2 oz beef fillet,
  cut into thin strips

250 ml/9 fl oz vegetable oil

3 celery stalks, cut into thin strips,
  2.5 cm/1 inch long

1 red pepper, cut into thin strips

1 red chilli, deseeded and finely
  sliced

lime wedges, to garnish

Thai fish sauce, to serve

Marinade

1 tsp salt

2 tbsp Thai fish sauce

Method

1 To make the marinade, mix the salt and fish sauce in a large bowl.

2 Add the beef to the marinade and toss to coat. Cover with clingfilm and place in the refrigerator for 1 hour to marinate.

3 Heat 225 ml/8 fl oz of the oil in a wok, add the beef and deep-fry over a medium heat for 2–3 minutes until crispy. Remove the wok from the heat and, using a slotted spoon, lift out the meat and drain it on kitchen paper. Discard all but 2 tablespoons of the oil.

4 Add the remaining oil to the wok. When it is hot add the celery, red pepper and chilli and stir-fry for 1 minute. Add the beef and cook until hot.

5 Garnish with lime wedges and serve with fish sauce.

33

Lamb with Black Bean Sauce

SERVES 4

450 g/1 lb lamb neck fillet or
  boneless leg of lamb chops

1 egg white, lightly beaten

4 tbsp cornflour

1 tsp Chinese five-spice powder

3 tbsp sunflower oil

1 red onion, sliced

1 red pepper, deseeded and sliced

1 green pepper, deseeded and sliced

1 yellow or orange pepper, deseeded
  and sliced

5 tbsp black bean sauce

cooked rice or noodles,
  to serve

Method

1 Using a sharp knife, slice the lamb into very thin strips.

2 Mix together the egg white, cornflour and Chinese five-spice powder. Toss the lamb strips in the mixture until evenly coated.

3 Heat the oil in a wok or frying pan and stir-fry the lamb over a high heat for 5 minutes or until it crispens around the edges.

4 Add the onion and pepper slices to the wok and stir-fry for 5–6 minutes, or until the vegetables just begin to soften.

5 Stir the black bean sauce into the mixture in the wok and heat through.

6 Transfer the lamb and sauce to warm serving plates and serve hot with freshly cooked rice or noodles.

34

Stir-fried Lamb with Orange

SERVES 4

450 g/1 lb fresh lamb mince

2 garlic cloves, crushed

1 tsp cumin seeds

1 tsp ground coriander

1 red onion, sliced

*finely grated rind and juice of
    1 orange*

2 tbsp soy sauce

1 orange, peeled and segmented

salt and pepper

*snipped fresh chives and strips of
    orange zest, to garnish*

Method

1 Heat a wok, without adding any oil. Add the lamb mince and dry-fry for 5 minutes, or until evenly browned. Drain away any excess fat from the wok.

2 Add the garlic, cumin seeds, coriander and red onion to the wok and stir-fry for a further 5 minutes.

3 Stir in the orange rind and juice and the soy sauce, mixing until thoroughly combined. Cover, reduce the heat and leave to simmer, stirring occasionally, for 15 minutes.

4 Remove the lid, increase the heat and add the orange segments. Stir to mix.

5 Season to taste with salt and pepper and heat through for a further 2–3 minutes. Transfer the stir-fry to warmed serving dishes and garnish with snipped chives and strips of orange zest. Serve immediately.

35

Green Lamb Stir-fry

SERVES 4

450 g/1 lb boneless lamb

2 tbsp soy sauce

2 tsp cornflour

200 ml/7 fl oz chicken stock

1 tbsp Thai fish sauce

100 g/3½ oz Chinese garlic chives,
   or green stalks from 2 bunches of
   spring onions

125 g/4½ oz dried egg noodles

3 tbsp groundnut oil

2-cm/¾-inch piece galangal or fresh
   ginger, finely chopped

5 tbsp green curry paste

50 g/1¾ oz dry-roasted peanuts,
   roughly chopped and juice of
   ½ lime, to garnish

salt

lime slices, to serve

Method

1 Slice the lamb into 4 x 1-cm/1½ x ½-inch strips and put in a shallow dish. Sprinkle with the soy sauce, cornflour and a pinch of salt, tossing well to coat. Cover and leave to marinate in the refrigerator for 1–24 hours.

2 Combine the stock, fish sauce and ½ teaspoon of salt. Trim the garlic chives and slice into 2-cm/¾-inch lengths.

3 Cook the noodles according to the packet instructions. Drain, return to the pan, and toss with 1 tablespoon of the oil.

4 Heat a wok over a high heat. Add the remaining oil and stir-fry the lamb for 3 minutes or until no longer pink. Add the galangal and curry paste and stir for another minute. Pour in the stock mixture and stir until boiling. Add the noodles, tossing to coat with the sauce. Add the chives and stir-fry for a few seconds until wilted. Garnish with the peanuts and lime juice, and serve at once with lime slices.

36

Red Lamb Curry

SERVES 4

2 tbsp vegetable oil

1 large onion, sliced

2 garlic cloves, crushed

500 g/1 lb 2 oz lean boneless leg
   of lamb, cut into 3-cm/1½-inch
   cubes

2 tbsp red curry paste

150 ml/5 fl oz coconut milk

1 tbsp soft light brown sugar

1 large red pepper, deseeded and
   thickly sliced

150 ml/5 fl oz lamb stock
   or beef stock

1 tbsp Thai fish sauce

2 tbsp lime juice

225 g/8 oz canned water chestnuts,
   drained

2 tbsp chopped fresh coriander

2 tbsp chopped fresh basil,
   plus extra leaves to garnish

salt and pepper

Method

1 Heat a wok over a high heat, then add the oil. Add the onion
and garlic and stir-fry for 2–3 minutes until soft. Add the lamb
and stir-fry quickly until lightly browned.

2 Stir in the curry paste and cook for a few seconds, then add the
coconut milk and sugar and bring to the boil. Reduce the heat and
leave to simmer for 15 minutes, stirring occasionally.

3 Stir in the red pepper, stock, fish sauce and lime juice, then cover
and simmer for a further 15 minutes, or until the lamb is tender.

4 Add the water chestnuts, coriander and chopped basil and
season to taste with salt and pepper. Transfer to serving plates,
then garnish with basil leaves and serve immediately.

37

Sweet & Sour Pork

SERVES 4

150 ml/5 fl oz vegetable oil,
   for deep-frying

225 g/8 oz pork fillet, cut into
   1-cm/½-inch cubes

1 onion, sliced

1 green pepper, deseeded and sliced

225 g/8 oz pineapple pieces

1 small carrot, cut into thin strips

25 g/1 oz canned bamboo shoots,
   drained, rinsed and halved

cooked rice or noodles, to serve

Batter

125 g/4½ oz plain flour

1 tbsp cornflour

1½ tsp baking powder

1 tbsp vegetable oil

Sauce

125 g/4½ oz soft light brown sugar

2 tbsp cornflour

125 ml/4 fl oz white wine vinegar

2 garlic cloves, crushed

4 tbsp tomato purée

Method

1 To make the batter, sift the plain flour into a mixing bowl, together with the cornflour and baking powder. Add the vegetable oil and stir in enough water to make a thick, smooth batter (about 175 ml/6 fl oz).

2 Pour the vegetable oil into a preheated wok and heat until almost smoking.

3 Dip the cubes of pork into the batter, and cook in the hot oil, in batches, until the pork is cooked through. Remove the pork from the wok with a slotted spoon and drain on kitchen paper. Set aside and keep warm until required.

4 Drain all but 1 tablespoon of oil from the wok and return it to the heat. Add the onion, pepper, pineapple pieces, carrot and bamboo shoots and stir-fry for 1–2 minutes. Remove from the wok with a slotted spoon and set aside. Mix all of the sauce ingredients together and pour into the wok.

5 Bring to the boil, stirring until thickened and clear. Cook for 1 minute, then return the pork and vegetables to the wok. Cook for a further 1–2 minutes, then transfer to a serving plate and serve with freshly cooked rice or noodles.

38

Honey-glazed Roast Pork

SERVES 4

2 tbsp clear honey

1 tbsp rice vinegar

2 tbsp light brown sugar

1 tbsp hoisin sauce

1 tbsp light soy sauce

2 tsp five-spice paste

500 g/1 lb 2 oz pork fillet,
     in one piece

3 tbsp rice wine

1 tsp cornflour

175 ml/6 fl oz chicken stock

stir-fried vegetables, to serve

Method

1 Mix the honey, vinegar, sugar, hoisin sauce, soy sauce and five-spice paste together in a wide non-metallic bowl. Pour over the pork. Cover and leave to marinate in the fridge overnight.

2 Preheat the oven to 200°C/400°F/Gas Mark 6. Drain the pork, reserving the marinade, and place on a wire rack in a roasting tin.

3 Pour a 2.5-cm/1-inch depth of boiling water into the tin and place in the oven for 20 minutes.

4 Turn the pork over, brush with the marinade, then cook for a further 20 minutes, or until there is no trace of pink in the juices.

5 Mix the rice wine and cornflour to a smooth paste, then place in a pan with the reserved marinade and stock.

6 Bring to boiling point, while stirring, then simmer for 2 minutes until thickened and clear.

7 Slice the pork thinly and serve with the sauce spooned over. Serve with stir-fried vegetables.

39

Pork with Basil & Lemon Grass

SERVES 4

350 g/12 oz pork tenderloin, cubed

2 tbsp sesame oil

280 g/10 oz mushrooms, thinly sliced

1 courgette, thinly sliced

2 carrots, thinly sliced

115 g/4 oz canned bamboo shoots, drained and rinsed

115 g/4 oz canned water chestnuts, thinly sliced

1 garlic clove, crushed

125 ml/4 fl oz chicken stock

lime wedges, to serve

cooked basmati rice, to serve

Marinade

1 lemon grass stalk, finely sliced

2 tbsp Thai fish sauce

4 tbsp fresh basil, shredded

juice of 1 lime

Method

1 To make the marinade, mix the lemon grass, fish sauce, basil and lime juice in a bowl. Stir in the pork and toss well to coat. Cover with clingfilm and refrigerate for 1–2 hours.

2 Heat 1 tablespoon of the oil in a preheated wok or frying pan over a medium heat. Add the meat and the marinade and stir-fry until the pork is browned. Remove from the pan, set aside and keep warm.

3 Add the remaining tablespoon of oil to the pan and heat. Add all the vegetables and the garlic and stir-fry for about 3 minutes.

4 Return the pork to the pan and add the chicken stock. Cook for 5 minutes until the stock is reduced.

5 Transfer the stir-fry to warmed serving dishes. Serve with lime wedges and freshly cooked basmati rice.

40

Pad Noodles with Pork & Prawns

SERVES 4

250 g/9 oz flat rice noodles

200 g/7 oz pork fillet

3 tbsp groundnut oil

2 shallots, finely chopped

2 garlic cloves, finely chopped

175 g/6 oz raw prawns, peeled and
    deveined

2 eggs, beaten

2 tbsp Thai fish sauce

juice of 1 lime

1 tbsp tomato ketchup

2 tsp light muscovado sugar

1/2 tsp dried chilli flakes

100 g/3 1/2 oz beansprouts

4 tbsp roasted salted peanuts,
    chopped

6 spring onions, diagonally sliced

Method

1 Soak the noodles in hot water for 10 minutes, or according to the packet instructions. Drain well.

2 Slice the pork into strips about 5 mm/¼ inch thick.

3 Heat the oil in a wok and stir-fry the shallots for 1–2 minutes, to soften.

4 Add the pork strips and stir-fry for 2–3 minutes.

5 Add the garlic and prawns and stir-fry for 1–2 minutes.

6 Pour in the beaten eggs and stir for a few seconds until lightly set.

7 Reduce the heat and add the noodles, fish sauce, lime juice, ketchup and sugar. Toss together and heat through.

8 Sprinkle with chilli flakes, beansprouts, peanuts and spring onions.

9 Transfer to bowls and serve.

41

Hoisin Pork with Garlic Noodles

SERVES 4

250 g/9 oz dried thick Chinese egg
  noodles, or Chinese wholemeal
  egg noodles

450 g/1 lb pork fillet, thinly sliced

1 tsp sugar

1 tbsp groundnut or corn oil

4 tbsp rice vinegar

4 tbsp white wine vinegar

4 tbsp hoisin sauce

2 spring onions, sliced diagonally

about 2 tbsp garlic-flavoured corn oil

2 large garlic cloves, thinly sliced

chopped fresh coriander, to garnish

Method

1 Boil the noodles for 3 minutes, until soft, or cook according to the packet instructions. Drain well, rinse under cold water and drain again, then set aside.

2 Meanwhile, sprinkle the pork slices with the sugar and use your hands to toss together. Heat a wok over a high heat. Add the oil and heat until it shimmers. Add the pork and stir-fry for about 3 minutes until the pork is cooked through and is no longer pink. Use a slotted spoon to remove the pork from the wok and keep warm. Add both vinegars to the wok and boil until they are reduced to about 5 tablespoons. Pour in the hoisin sauce with the spring onions and let it bubble until reduced by half. Add to the pork and stir together.

3 Quickly wipe out the wok and reheat. Add the garlic-flavoured oil and heat until it shimmers. Add the garlic slices and stir round for about 30 seconds, until they are golden and crisp, then use a slotted spoon to scoop them out of the wok and set aside.

4 Add the noodles to the wok and stir them round to warm them through. Divide the noodles between 4 plates, top with the pork and onion mixture and garnish with the garlic slices and coriander.

42

Ginger Pork with Mushrooms

SERVES 4

2 tbsp vegetable oil

3 shallots, finely chopped

2 garlic cloves, crushed

5-cm/2-inch piece fresh ginger,
   thinly sliced

500 g/1 lb 2 oz pork stir-fry strips

250 g/9 oz shiitake mushrooms,
   sliced

4 tbsp soy sauce

4 tbsp rice wine

1 tsp light muscovado sugar

1 tsp cornflour

2 tbsp cold water

3 tbsp chopped fresh coriander,
   to garnish

Method

1 Heat the oil in a wok and fry the shallots for 2–3 minutes,
to soften.

2 Add the garlic and ginger and stir-fry for 1 minute.

3 Add the pork strips and stir-fry for 1 minute.

4 Add the mushrooms and stir-fry for a further 2–3 minutes.

5 Stir in the soy sauce, rice wine and sugar.

6 Blend the cornflour and water until smooth, add to the pan,
stirring, and cook until the juices are thickened and clear.

7 Serve the stir-fry garnished with coriander.

3

POULTRY

43

Green Chicken Curry

SERVES 4

2 tbsp groundnut oil or sunflower oil

2 tbsp green curry paste

500 g/1 lb 2 oz skinless, boneless
chicken breasts, cut into cubes

2 kaffir lime leaves, roughly torn

1 lemon grass stalk, finely chopped

225 ml/8 fl oz coconut milk

16 baby aubergines, halved

2 tbsp Thai fish sauce

fresh Thai basil sprigs and thinly
sliced kaffir lime leaves, to garnish

Method

1 Heat the oil in a preheated wok or large, heavy-based frying pan. Add the curry paste and stir-fry briefly until all the aromas are released.

2 Add the chicken, lime leaves and lemon grass and stir-fry for 3–4 minutes, until the meat is beginning to colour. Add the coconut milk and aubergines and simmer gently for 8–10 minutes, or until tender.

3 Stir in the fish sauce and serve immediately, garnished with basil sprigs and sliced lime leaves.

44

Chicken Chow Mein

SERVES 4

250 g/9 oz medium egg noodles

2 tbsp sunflower oil

275 g/9¾ oz cooked chicken breasts, shredded

1 garlic clove, finely chopped

1 red pepper, deseeded and thinly sliced

100 g/3½ oz shiitake mushrooms, sliced

6 spring onions, sliced

100 g/3½ oz beansprouts

3 tbsp soy sauce

1 tbsp sesame oil

Method

1 Place the egg noodles in a large bowl or dish and break them up slightly. Pour enough boiling water over the noodles to cover and leave to stand while preparing the other ingredients.

2 Heat the sunflower oil in a large preheated wok. Add the chicken, garlic, red pepper, mushrooms, spring onions and beansprouts to the wok and stir-fry for about 5 minutes.

3 Drain the noodles thoroughly. Add the noodles to the wok, toss well and stir-fry for a further 5 minutes.

4 Drizzle the soy sauce and sesame oil over the chow mein and toss until well combined.

5 Transfer to warmed serving bowls and serve immediately.

45

Chicken with Cashew Nuts

SERVES 4–6

450 g/1 lb boneless chicken meat,
  cut into bite-sized pieces

3 tbsp light soy sauce

1 tsp Shaoxing rice wine

pinch of sugar

1/2 tsp salt

3 dried Chinese mushrooms, soaked
  in warm water for 20 minutes

2 tbsp vegetable or groundnut oil

4 slices of fresh ginger

1 tsp finely chopped garlic

1 red pepper, deseeded and cut into
  2.5-cm/1-inch squares

85 g/3 oz cashew nuts, toasted

Method

1 Marinate the chicken in 2 tablespoons of the light soy sauce, Shaoxing, sugar and salt for at least 20 minutes.

2 Squeeze any excess water from the mushrooms and finely slice, discarding any tough stems. Reserve the soaking water.

3 In a preheated wok, heat 1 tablespoon of the oil. Add the ginger and stir-fry until fragrant. Stir in the chicken and cook for 2 minutes, until it turns brown. Before the chicken is cooked through, remove and set aside.

4 Clean the wok, heat the remaining oil and stir-fry the garlic until fragrant. Add the mushrooms and red pepper and stir-fry for 1 minute.

5 Add about 2 tablespoons of the mushroom soaking water and cook for about 2 minutes until the water has evaporated.

6 Return the chicken to the wok, add the remaining light soy sauce and the cashew nuts and stir-fry for 2 minutes until the chicken is cooked through.

7 Transfer to bowls and serve.

46

Sweet & Sour Chicken

SERVES 4–6

450 g/1 lb lean chicken, cubed

5 tbsp vegetable or groundnut oil

1/2 tsp crushed garlic

1/2 tsp finely chopped fresh ginger

1 green pepper, deseeded and
    roughly chopped

1 onion, roughly chopped

1 carrot, finely sliced

1 tsp sesame oil

1 tbsp finely chopped spring onion

freshly cooked rice, to serve

Marinade

2 tsp light soy sauce

1 tsp Chinese rice wine

pinch of white pepper

1/2 tsp salt

dash of sesame oil

Sauce

8 tbsp rice vinegar

4 tbsp sugar

2 tsp light soy sauce

6 tbsp tomato ketchup

Method

1 Combine all the marinade ingredients in a bowl and marinate the chicken pieces for at least 20 minutes.

2 To prepare the sauce, heat the vinegar in a pan and add the sugar, light soy sauce and tomato ketchup. Stir to dissolve the sugar, then set aside.

3 In a preheated wok or large frying pan, heat 3 tablespoons of the oil and stir-fry the chicken until it starts to turn golden brown. Remove and set aside. Wipe the wok clean.

4 In the clean wok, heat the remaining oil and cook the garlic and ginger until fragrant. Add the vegetables and cook for 2 minutes. Add the chicken and cook for 1 minute. Finally add the sauce and the sesame oil, then stir in the spring onion and serve immediately with freshly cooked rice.

47

Yaki Soba

SERVES 2

400 g/14 oz ramen noodles

1 onion, finely sliced

200 g/7 oz beansprouts

1 red pepper, deseeded and sliced

150 g/5½ oz chicken,
  cooked and sliced

12 cooked peeled prawns

1 tbsp oil, for stir-frying

2 tbsp shoyu

½ tbsp mirin

1 tsp sesame oil

1 tsp sesame seeds and 2 spring
  onions, finely sliced, to garnish

Method

1 Cook the noodles according to the packet instructions, drain well, and tip into a bowl.

2 Mix the onion, beansprouts, red pepper, chicken and prawns together in a bowl. Stir through the noodles. Meanwhile, preheat a wok over a high heat, add the oil and heat until very hot.

3 Add the noodle mixture and stir-fry for 4 minutes, or until golden, then add the shoyu, mirin and sesame oil and toss together.

4 Divide the noodles between two bowls.

5 Sprinkle with sesame seeds and spring onions and serve.

48

Peppered Chicken Stir-fry

SERVES 4–6

4 tsp soy sauce

1 tbsp cornflour

1 tbsp Chinese rice wine
  or dry sherry

1/4 tsp salt

350 g/12 oz skinless, boneless
  chicken breasts, cut into cubes

6 tbsp chicken stock

1 tbsp oyster sauce

4 tbsp groundnut or vegetable oil

1 tsp finely chopped fresh ginger

1 large garlic clove, thinly sliced

4 spring onions, white and green
  parts separated, diagonally sliced
  into 2-cm/3/4-inch pieces

1/2 tbsp white peppercorns, crushed

8 baby corn, diagonally halved

1/2 small red pepper, deseeded and
  thinly sliced

140 g/5 oz canned water chestnuts,
  drained

115 g/4 oz mangetout,
  diagonally halved

Method

1 In a small bowl, combine half the soy sauce, the cornflour, rice wine and salt. Put the chicken pieces in a shallow dish and pour over the soy sauce mixture, stirring to coat. Leave to stand for 15 minutes.

2 Mix the remaining soy sauce with the stock and oyster sauce, and set aside.

3 Heat a wok over a high heat, then add the oil. Add the chicken and stir-fry for 3 minutes, until no longer pink. Remove from the wok with a slotted spoon and drain on kitchen paper.

4 Reduce the heat slightly, then add the ginger, garlic, white spring onions and the crushed peppercorns and stir for a few seconds. Add the baby corn, red pepper and water chestnuts. Stir-fry for 2 minutes, then return the chicken to the wok. Add the mangetout and the soy sauce mixture and stir-fry for 1–2 minutes, until the sauce is thickened.

5 Sprinkle with the green spring onion and cook for a few more seconds. Serve immediately.

49

Teriyaki Chicken

SERVES 4

4 boneless chicken breasts,
  about 175 g/6 oz each, with or
  without skin

4 tbsp bottled teriyaki sauce

peanut or corn oil, for brushing

Sesame noodles

250 g/9 oz dried thin buckwheat
  noodles

1 tbsp toasted sesame oil

2 tbsp sesame seeds, toasted

2 tbsp finely chopped fresh parsley

salt and pepper

Method

1 Using a sharp knife score each chicken breast diagonally across 3 times. Rub all over with teriyaki sauce. Set aside in the refrigerator to marinate for at least 10 minutes and up to 24 hours.

2 Preheat the grill to high. Bring a saucepan of water to the boil, add the buckwheat noodles and cook according to the packet instructions. Drain and rinse well in cold water.

3 Lightly brush the griddle pan with oil. Add the chicken breasts, skin side up.

4 Griddle the chicken breast, brushing occasionally with extra teriyaki sauce, for 15 minutes, or until cooked through and the juices run clear when pierced with a skewer.

5 Meanwhile, heat a wok over high heat. Add the sesame oil and heat until it shimmers.

6 Add the noodles and stir round to heat through, then stir in the sesame seeds and parsley. Add salt and pepper to taste. Transfer the chicken breasts to plates and add a portion of noodles to each.

50

Gong Bau Chicken

SERVES 4

2 boneless chicken breasts, with or without skin, cut into 1-cm/ 1/2-inch cubes

1 tbsp vegetable or groundnut oil

10 dried red chillies or more, to taste, snipped into 2–3 pieces

1 tsp Szechuan peppers

3 garlic cloves, finely sliced

2.5-cm/1-inch piece fresh ginger, finely sliced

1 tbsp roughly chopped spring onion, white part only

85 g/3 oz peanuts, roasted

Marinade

2 tsp light soy sauce

1 tsp Chinese rice wine

1/2 tsp sugar

Sauce

1 tsp light soy sauce

1 tsp dark soy sauce

1 tsp black rice vinegar

a few drops of sesame oil

2 tbsp chicken stock

1 tsp sugar

Method

1 Combine all the marinade ingredients in a bowl and marinate the chicken, covered, for at least 20 minutes. Combine all the ingredients for the sauce and set aside.

2 In a preheated wok or large frying pan, heat the oil and stir-fry the chillies and peppers until crisp and fragrant. Toss in the chicken pieces. When they begin to turn white, add the garlic, ginger and spring onion. Stir-fry for about 5 minutes, or until the chicken is cooked.

3 Pour in the sauce, mix together thoroughly, then stir in the peanuts. Serve immediately.

51

Chicken with Pistachio Nuts

SERVES 4

50 ml/2 fl oz chicken stock

2 tbsp soy sauce

2 tbsp dry sherry

3 tsp cornflour

1 egg white, beaten

1/2 tsp salt

4 tbsp groundnut or vegetable oil

450 g/1 lb chicken breast,
    cut into strips

450 g/1 lb mushrooms, thinly sliced

1 head of broccoli, cut into florets

150 g/51/2 oz beansprouts

100 g/31/2 oz canned water
    chestnuts, drained and
    thinly sliced

175 g/6 oz pistachio nuts,
    plus extra to garnish

cooked rice, to serve

Method

1 Combine the chicken stock, soy sauce and sherry with 1 teaspoon of cornflour. Stir well and set aside.

2 Combine the egg white, salt, 2 tablespoons of the oil and 2 teaspoons of cornflour. Toss and coat the chicken in the mixture.

3 In a wok or frying pan, heat the remaining oil until hot. Add the chicken in batches and stir-fry until golden. Remove from the wok, drain on kitchen paper and set aside to keep warm.

4 Add more oil to the wok if needed and stir-fry the mushrooms, then add the broccoli and cook for 2–3 minutes.

5 Return the chicken to the wok and add the beansprouts, water chestnuts and pistachio nuts. Stir-fry until all the ingredients are thoroughly warm. Add the chicken stock mixture and cook, stirring continuously until thickened.

6 Serve immediately over a bed of freshly cooked rice, garnished with pistachios.

52

Spice Chicken with Courgettes

SERVES 4

1 tbsp groundnut oil

1 clove garlic, finely chopped

2.5 cm/1 in piece fresh ginger, finely chopped

1 small fresh red chilli, deseeded and finely chopped

350 g/12 oz skinless boneless chicken breasts, cut into thin strips

1 tbsp seven-spice powder

1 red pepper, deseeded and sliced

1 yellow pepper, deseeded and sliced

2 courgettes, thinly sliced

225 g/8 oz canned bamboo shoots, drained

2 tbsp dry sherry or apple juice

1 tbsp light soy sauce

2 tbsp chopped fresh coriander, plus extra to garnish

salt and pepper

Method

1 Heat the oil in a non-stick wok or large frying pan. Add the garlic, ginger and chilli and stir-fry for 30 seconds to release the flavours.

2 Add the chicken and seven-spice powder and stir-fry for about 4 minutes, or until the chicken has coloured all over. Add the red pepper, yellow pepper and courgettes and stir-fry for 1–2 minutes, or until slightly soft.

3 Stir in the bamboo shoots and stir-fry for a further 2–3 minutes, or until the chicken is cooked through and tender. Add the sherry and soy sauce, season to taste with salt and pepper and sizzle for 1–2 minutes.

4 Stir in the coriander and serve immediately, garnished with extra coriander.

53

Chicken Fried Rice

SERVES 4

1/2 tbsp sesame oil

6 shallots, peeled and quartered

450 g/1 lb cooked, cubed chicken meat

3 tbsp soy sauce

2 carrots, diced

1 stalk celery, diced

1 red pepper, deseeded and diced

175 g/6 oz fresh peas

100 g/3 1/2 oz canned sweetcorn kernels

275 g/9 3/4 oz cooked long-grain rice

2 large eggs, scrambled

Method

1 Heat the oil in a large wok or frying pan over a medium heat. Add the shallots and fry until soft, then add the chicken and 2 tablespoons of the soy sauce and stir-fry for 5–6 minutes.

2 Stir in the carrots, celery, red pepper, peas and sweetcorn and stir-fry for another 5 minutes. Add the rice and stir thoroughly.

3 Finally stir in the scrambled eggs and the remaining soy sauce. Serve immediately.

54

Ginger Chicken with Noodles

SERVES 4

2 tbsp vegetable oil or groundnut oil

1 onion, sliced

2 garlic cloves, finely chopped

5-cm/2-inch piece fresh ginger,
thinly sliced

2 carrots, thinly sliced

4 skinless, boneless chicken breasts,
cut into cubes

300 ml/10 fl oz chicken stock

4 tbsp Thai soy sauce

225 g/8 oz canned bamboo shoots,
drained and rinsed

75 g/2¾ oz flat rice noodles

4 chopped spring onions and
4 tbsp chopped fresh coriander,
to garnish

Method

1 Heat the oil in a wok and stir-fry the onion, garlic, ginger and carrots for 1–2 minutes until soft. Add the chicken and stir-fry for 3–4 minutes, until the chicken is cooked through and lightly browned.

2 Add the stock, soy sauce and bamboo shoots and gradually bring to the boil. Simmer for 2–3 minutes.

3 Meanwhile, bring a saucepan of water to the boil, add the noodles and soak for 6–8 minutes. Drain well, then garnish with the spring onions and coriander. Serve immediately with the chicken stir-fry.

55

Turkey Teriyaki

SERVES 4

450 g/1 lb turkey steaks,
   cut into strips

3 tbsp groundnut oil

1 small yellow pepper, deseeded and
   sliced into thin strips

8 spring onions, green part included,
   diagonally sliced into 2.5-cm/
   1-inch pieces

freshly cooked plain rice, to serve

Teriyaki glaze

5 tbsp shoyu (Japanese soy sauce)

5 tbsp mirin

2 tbsp clear honey

1 tsp finely chopped fresh ginger

Method

1 Mix the glaze ingredients in a small saucepan over low–medium heat. Stir until the honey has melted, then remove from the heat and leave to cool.

2 Put the turkey in a large shallow dish. Pour over the glaze, turning the strips so they are well coated. Leave to marinate for 30 minutes at room temperature, or overnight in the refrigerator.

3 Using a slotted spoon, remove the turkey from the marinade, shaking off the excess liquid. Reserve the marinade.

4 Heat a wok over a medium–high heat, then add the oil. Add the turkey and stir-fry for 2 minutes. Add the yellow pepper and spring onions, and fry for 1 minute. Pour in the reserved marinade. Bring to the boil, then reduce the heat slightly and cook for 3–4 minutes, until the turkey is cooked through.

5 Transfer the turkey and vegetables to a warmed serving dish. Boil the liquid remaining in the wok until syrupy, then pour over the turkey. Serve immediately with rice.

56

Turkey with Pak Choi

SERVES 4

225 g/8 oz medium egg noodles

3 tbsp groundnut oil

1 large garlic clove, thinly sliced

2 tsp finely chopped fresh ginger

450 g/1 lb turkey steaks,
    cut into thin strips

175 g/6 oz chestnut mushrooms,
    thinly sliced

600 g/1 lb 5 oz pak choi, stalks cut
    into 2.5-cm/1-inch squares and
    leaves sliced into wide ribbons

4 spring onions, green part included,
    diagonally sliced into 2.5-cm/
    1-inch pieces

1 tbsp light soy sauce

2 tbsp chopped fresh coriander

salt and pepper

Method

1 Cook the noodles in a saucepan of boiling water for 4 minutes, or according to the instructions on the packet, until soft. Drain, rinse and drain again, then leave to cool.

2 Heat a wok over a medium–high heat, then add the oil. Stir-fry the garlic and ginger for a few seconds to flavour the oil.

3 Add the turkey and stir-fry for 2 minutes, until no longer pink. Add the mushrooms and pak choi stalks, and stir-fry for 2 minutes. Add the pak choi leaves and spring onions, and stir-fry for a further 2 minutes. Stir in the noodles and soy sauce, and season to taste with salt and pepper. Cook until the noodles are heated through, then add the coriander. Serve immediately.

57

Turkey with Hoisin Sauce

SERVES 4

450 g/1 lb turkey steaks, cubed

4 tbsp groundnut oil

3 large garlic cloves, thinly sliced

4 spring onions, white and green
parts separated, diagonally sliced
into 2-cm/3⁄4-inch pieces

1 tbsp Chinese rice wine
or dry sherry

3 tbsp hoisin sauce

4 tbsp cashew nuts

Marinade

1 tsp cornflour

1 tbsp Chinese rice wine
or dry sherry

1⁄4 tsp white pepper

1⁄2 tsp salt

1⁄2 egg white, lightly beaten

2 tsp sesame oil

Method

1 To make the marinade, mix the cornflour and rice wine to a paste. Add the pepper, salt, egg white and sesame oil, mixing well. Put the turkey in a shallow dish and add the marinade, turning to coat. Leave to stand for 30 minutes.

2 Heat a wok over a high heat, then add 3 tablespoons of the groundnut oil. Add the garlic and white spring onions, and stir for a few seconds to flavour the oil. Add the turkey and reduce the heat slightly. Stir-fry for 2 minutes, until no longer pink, then sprinkle with the rice wine. Transfer to a plate with a slotted spoon.

3 Increase the heat to high and add the remaining groundnut oil. Swirl the oil around the wok, then stir in the hoisin sauce. Return the turkey mixture to the wok and stir-fry for 2–3 minutes, turning to coat, until cooked through.

4 Add the cashew nuts and green spring onion. Transfer to a warmed serving dish and serve immediately.

58

Lemon Turkey with Spinach

SERVES 4

450 g/1 lb turkey breast,
  cut into strips

1 tbsp vegetable oil

6 spring onions, finely sliced

1/2 lemon, peeled and thinly sliced

1 garlic clove, finely chopped

300 g/10 1/2 oz spinach, washed,
  drained and roughly chopped

3 tbsp chopped fresh
  flat-leaf parsley

sprigs of flat-leaf parsley and lemon
  slices, to garnish

cooked pasta, to serve

Marinade

1 tbsp soy sauce

1 tbsp white wine vinegar

1 tsp cornflour

1 tsp finely grated lemon zest

1/2 tsp finely ground black pepper

Method

1 To make the marinade, put the soy sauce, vinegar, cornflour, lemon zest and pepper in a bowl and mix thoroughly. Add the turkey and stir to coat. Cover with clingfilm and marinate in the refrigerator for 30 minutes.

2 Heat the oil in a large wok or frying pan. Add the turkey and the marinade and cook over a medium heat for 2–3 minutes or until the turkey is opaque.

3 Add the spring onions, lemon slices and garlic and cook for another 2–3 minutes. Stir in the spinach and parsley and cook until the spinach is just wilted.

4 Remove from the heat, spoon over freshly cooked pasta and garnish with sprigs of parsley and lemon slices before serving.

59

Duck with Mixed Peppers

SERVES 4

1 tbsp vegetable or groundnut oil

2 boneless duck breasts, skin on, weighing about 550 g/1 lb 4 oz in total

1 onion, sliced

2 garlic cloves, chopped

1 red pepper, deseeded and sliced

1 green pepper, deseeded and sliced

1 yellow pepper, deseeded and sliced

4 tomatoes, peeled, deseeded and chopped

150 ml/5 fl oz stock

3 tbsp Thai soy sauce

freshly cooked noodles sprinkled with spring onions, to serve

Method

1 Heat a wok over a high heat, then add the oil. Cook the duck, skin-side down, for 5–10 minutes, or until crisp and brown. Turn over and cook for a further 5 minutes, until cooked through. Remove the duck from the wok and keep warm.

2 Pour off any excess fat and stir-fry the onion and garlic for 2–3 minutes, until softened and lightly browned.

3 Add the peppers and stir-fry for 2–3 minutes, until tender. Add the tomatoes, stock and soy sauce, and simmer for 1–2 minutes. Transfer to a serving plate. Slice the duck thickly and arrange on top, spooning any sauce over it. Serve with noodles.

60

Cantonese Sweet & Sour Duck

SERVES 6

2 boneless duck breasts, skin on,
 weighing about 550 g/1 lb 4 oz
 in total

1/2 tbsp soy sauce

2 tsp groundnut oil

salt and pepper

4-cm/1 1/2-inch piece cucumber,
 peeled and sliced lengthways into
 matchsticks, to garnish

Sauce

1 tbsp cornflour

125 ml/4 fl oz chicken stock

1 1/2 tbsp soy sauce

1 1/2 tbsp rice vinegar

2 tbsp sugar

1 tbsp tomato purée

1 tbsp orange juice

2 tsp groundnut oil

3 thin slices fresh ginger

Method

1 Slice each duck breast into 3 pieces and put in a dish. Rub with salt and pepper and the half tablespoon of soy sauce.

2 Heat a wok over a medium–high heat, then add the oil. Fry the duck for 6 minutes, starting with the skin side down, and turning until brown and crisp on all sides. Using tongs, transfer to a plate and leave to rest in a warm place for 10 minutes. Discard the oil and wipe the wok clean with kitchen paper. Slice the duck into 1-cm/1/2-inch strips (the meat will still be quite rare at this stage).

3 To prepare the sauce, mix the cornflour to a smooth paste with 3 tablespoons of the stock. Combine the soy sauce, vinegar and sugar in a small bowl, stirring to dissolve the sugar. Add the tomato purée and orange juice, mixing well.

4 Heat the oil in the clean wok over a medium heat. Add the ginger slices and stir-fry for a few seconds to flavour the oil. Add the soy sauce mixture and the remaining stock, and bring to the boil. Reduce the heat slightly and add in the cornflour paste. Stir until starting to thicken, then add the duck slices, stirring to coat with the sauce. Simmer over a low heat for 5 minutes, until the duck is cooked but still slightly pink.

5 Remove the ginger slices and transfer the duck and sauce to a warmed serving dish. Garnish with the cucumber and serve immediately.

61

Duck with Black Beans

SERVES 2–3

2 small duck breasts, weighing
  450 g/1 lb in total

2 tbsp salted black beans

1 1/2 tbsp soy sauce

1 tbsp rice vinegar

2 tsp sugar

200 g/7 oz broccoli

3 tbsp groundnut oil

2.5-cm/1-inch piece fresh ginger,
  cut into very thin shreds

1 fresh red chilli, deseeded and
  thinly sliced diagonally

1 large garlic clove, thinly sliced

1/2 red pepper, deseeded and thinly
  sliced

Method

1 Remove and discard the skin from the duck. Slice the meat into 5-mm/1/4-inch strips.

2 Soak the beans in cold water for 30 minutes, then drain. Combine the soy sauce, vinegar and sugar in a small bowl, stirring to dissolve the sugar.

3 Divide the broccoli into florets. Slice the stems very thinly and slice the florets into pieces no more than 2 cm/3/4 inch wide.

4 Heat a wok over a medium heat, then add the oil. Fry the ginger, chilli and garlic for a few seconds to flavour the oil. Add the drained beans, broccoli and red pepper. Increase the heat to high and stir-fry for 2 minutes.

5 Add the duck and stir-fry for 2 minutes, then add the soy sauce mixture. Continue to stir-fry for a further 2 minutes. Serve immediately.

62

Three-pea Stir-fry with Duck

SERVES 4

2 small skinless, boneless duck
    breasts, weighing about
    450 g/1 lb in total

3 tbsp groundnut oil

6 large spring onions, white and
    green parts separated, diagonally
    sliced into 2-cm/3⁄4-inch pieces

1 tsp finely chopped fresh ginger

175 g/6 oz sugar snap peas

115 g/4 oz mangetout, diagonally
    sliced in half

140 g/5 oz shelled peas

3 tbsp whole almonds with skin,
    halved lengthways

55 g/2 oz fresh beansprouts

freshly cooked noodles, to serve

Marinade

1 tbsp light brown sugar

3 tbsp warm water

1–2 fresh red chillies, deseeded and
    very finely chopped

1 tbsp soy sauce

1 tsp Thai fish sauce

3 tbsp lime juice

Method

1 Combine the marinade ingredients in a bowl, stirring to
dissolve the sugar. Slice the duck into bite-sized pieces and
add to the marinade. Leave to stand at room temperature for
30 minutes, or overnight in the refrigerator.

2 Heat a wok over a high heat, then add the oil. Stir-fry the
white spring onion and the ginger for a few seconds. Add the
duck and the marinade, and stir-fry for about 5 minutes. When
the liquid has reduced slightly, add the three types of pea and
stir-fry for a further 2–3 minutes.

3 Add the almonds, beansprouts and green spring onion, and
stir-fry for a few seconds to heat through. Serve with noodles.

4

FISH & SEAFOOD

63

Thai Green Fish Curry

SERVES 4

2 tbsp vegetable oil

1 garlic clove, chopped

2 tbsp Thai green curry paste

1 small aubergine, diced

125 ml/4 fl oz coconut milk

2 tbsp Thai fish sauce

1 tsp sugar

225 g/8 oz firm white fish fillets,
   cut into pieces

125 ml/4 fl oz fish stock

2 kaffir lime leaves, finely shredded

about 15 fresh Thai basil leaves

sprigs of fresh dill, to garnish

Method

1 Heat the vegetable oil in a large frying pan or preheated wok over a medium heat until almost smoking. Add the garlic and cook until golden. Add the curry paste and stir-fry a few seconds before adding the aubergine. Stir-fry for about 4–5 minutes until softened.

2 Add the coconut milk, bring to the boil and stir until it thickens and curdles slightly. Add the fish sauce and sugar to the frying pan and stir well.

3 Add the fish pieces and stock. Simmer for 3–4 minutes, stirring occasionally, until the fish is just tender. Add the lime leaves and basil, then cook for a further 1 minute. Transfer to a warmed serving dish and garnish with a few sprigs of fresh dill. Serve immediately.

64

Fried Fish with Pine Nuts

SERVES 4–6

1/2 tsp salt

450 g/1 lb thick white fish fillets,
   cut into 2.5-cm/1-inch cubes

2 dried Chinese mushrooms, soaked
   in warm water for 20 minutes

3 tbsp vegetable or groundnut oil

2.5-cm/1-inch piece of fresh ginger,
   finely shredded

1 tbsp chopped spring onion

1 red pepper, cut into
   2.5-cm/1-inch squares

1 green pepper, cut into 2.5-cm/
   1-inch squares

25 g/1 oz fresh or canned bamboo
   shoots, rinsed and cut into small
   cubes (if using fresh shoots, boil
   in water first for 30 minutes)

2 tsp Shaoxing rice wine

2 tbsp pine nuts, toasted

cooked rice, to serve

Method

1 Sprinkle the salt over the fish and set aside for 20 minutes.
Squeeze out any excess water from the mushrooms and slice finely,
discarding any tough stems.

2 In a preheated wok, heat 2 tablespoons of the oil and fry the
fish for 3 minutes. Drain the fish, set aside and then wipe the
wok clean.

3 Preheat the clean wok and heat the remaining oil and toss
in the ginger. Stir until fragrant, then add the spring onion,
pepper, bamboo shoots, mushrooms and Shaoxing and cook for
1–2 minutes.

4 Finally add the fish and stir to warm through. Sprinkle with pine
nuts and serve with freshly cooked rice.

65

Rice Noodles with Yellow Fish

SERVES 6

225 g/8 oz dried fine rice noodles

70 g/2 1/2 oz rice flour or plain flour

1/2 tsp ground turmeric

900 g/2 lb white fish fillets, such as
tilapia or flounder, cut into
2-cm/3/4-inch cubes

2 tbsp groundnut or vegetable oil,
plus extra for deep-frying

4 spring onions, cut into 2.5-cm/
1-inch lengths

50 g/1 3/4 oz dry-roasted
unsalted peanuts

24 fresh Thai basil leaves

24 fresh dill sprigs, trimmed

24 fresh coriander sprigs, trimmed

salt and pepper

Method

1 Cook the noodles according to the packet instructions, until tender. Transfer to individual serving dishes.

2 Put the flour and turmeric in a sealable polythene bag and season to taste with salt and pepper. Shake to mix well. Add the fish cubes, then seal the bag and shake to coat each fish cube evenly.

3 Heat enough oil for deep-frying in a wok to 180–190°C/350–375°F, or until a cube of bread browns in 30 seconds. Working in small batches, take a handful of fish cubes and shake off the excess flour, then lower into the hot oil. Deep-fry for 2–3 minutes, or until golden and crisp. Drain on kitchen paper. Divide the fried fish cubes equally among the serving dishes.

4 Heat a clean wok over a high heat, then add the 2 tablespoons of oil. Add the spring onions and peanuts and stir-fry for 1 minute. Add the basil, dill and coriander and stir-fry for 1–2 minutes, or until just wilted. Divide among the serving dishes and serve immediately.

66

Cod with Spiced Noodles

SERVES 4

2 tbsp groundnut or vegetable oil,
    plus extra for brushing

juice and finely grated rind of
    1 large lemon

4 cod or haddock steaks,
    about 140 g/5 oz each, skinned

paprika, to taste

salt and pepper

Spiced noodles

250 g/9 oz dried medium
    egg noodles

2 garlic cloves, chopped

2.5-cm/1-inch piece fresh ginger,
    finely chopped

2 tbsp very finely chopped fresh
    coriander root

1 tbsp kecap manis
    (sweet soy sauce)

1 fresh red bird's eye chilli,
    deseeded and finely chopped

1 tbsp Thai fish sauce

Method

1 Preheat the grill to high. Put the noodles in a saucepan of boiling water and cook for 3 minutes, or cook according to the packet instructions, until tender. Drain, rinse with cold water and drain again, then set aside.

2 Mix 1 tablespoon of the oil with the lemon juice and brush over one side of each fish steak. Sprinkle with the lemon rind and paprika and season to taste with salt and pepper. Lightly brush a grill rack with oil, then place the fish on the rack and cook under the preheated grill for 8–10 minutes, until the flesh flakes easily.

3 Meanwhile, heat a wok over a high heat, then add the remaining oil. Add the garlic and ginger and stir-fry for about 30 seconds. Add the coriander root and kecap manis and stir around. Add the noodles and stir thoroughly so they are coated in the kecap manis. Stir in the chilli and fish sauce. Divide the spiced noodles among individual serving plates, top each with a fish steak and serve immediately.

67

Fish with Tomatoes & Herbs

SERVES 6

140 g/5 oz plain flour

*6 flounder or tilapia fillets,
about 175 g/6 oz each*

4–6 tbsp groundnut or vegetable oil

2 large garlic cloves, thinly sliced

4 ripe tomatoes, quartered

1 tbsp Thai fish sauce

12 fresh dill sprigs, trimmed

12 fresh coriander sprigs, trimmed

12 fresh Thai basil leaves

salt and pepper

*rice and sweet and sour fish sauce,
to serve*

Method

1 Put the flour in a sealable polythene bag with salt and pepper to taste. Add the fish. Seal the bag and toss the fish gently to coat with flour.

2 Heat 2 tablespoons of oil in a frying pan over a high heat. Working in batches and adding extra oil as needed, fry the fillets for 5–7 minutes, or until golden and crisp on both sides. Transfer to a serving platter.

3 Heat a wok over a high heat, then add 1 tablespoon of oil. Add the garlic and stir-fry for 3–5 minutes, or until just golden. Add the tomatoes and fish sauce and stir-fry for 10 minutes, or until softened. Adjust the seasoning, adding salt and pepper if needed. Spoon the tomato mixture on top of the fish.

4 Wipe out the wok with kitchen paper, then heat 1 tablespoon of oil over a high heat. Add the dill, coriander and basil and stir-fry for 1–2 minutes, or until just wilted. Scatter the herbs over the tomatoes and fish. Serve with rice and sweet and sour fish sauce.

68

Prawns Fu Yung

SERVES 4–6

1 tbsp vegetable or groundnut oil

115 g/4 oz large prawns, peeled and deveined

4 eggs, lightly beaten

1 tsp salt

pinch of white pepper

2 tbsp finely chopped Chinese chives

Method

1 Heat a wok over a high heat and add the oil. Add the prawns and stir-fry for about 4 minutes, or until just pink.

2 Season the eggs with the salt and pepper and pour over the prawns. Stir-fry for 1 minute, then add the chives.

3 Cook for a further 4 minutes, stirring all the time, until the eggs are cooked through but still soft in texture. Serve immediately.

69

Steamed Salmon with Asparagus

SERVES 4

4 salmon steaks, about
   2.5 cm/1 inch thick

2 tsp finely chopped fresh ginger

2 tbsp Chinese rice wine
   or dry sherry

1 tbsp light soy sauce

1/2 tsp salt

8 asparagus spears

4 tbsp groundnut oil

3 heads pak choi,
   quartered lengthways

good squeeze of lime juice

2 tsp sesame oil

pepper

freshly cooked plain rice, to serve

Method

1 Place the salmon steaks in a single layer on a heatproof plate that will fit into a wok. Combine the ginger, wine, soy sauce and salt. Sprinkle this over the fish, rubbing it into the flesh, and leave to stand for 20 minutes, turning once.

2 Snap the woody ends from the asparagus and discard. Cut off the tips and reserve. Chop the stems into 2 or 3 pieces.

3 Place a trivet in a wok with a lid, and add enough water to come halfway up the trivet. Bring to the boil, then place the plate of fish on the trivet and cover with a loose tent of foil. Adjust the heat so the water is only just boiling. Put the lid on the wok and steam for 10–15 minutes until the fish is opaque and just starting to flake.

4 Meanwhile, heat a second wok over high heat, then add 2 tablespoons of the groundnut oil. Add the asparagus stalks and pak choi, and stir-fry for 4–5 minutes until just tender but still crisp. Splash with a good squeeze of lime juice and season with salt and pepper. Arrange in small mounds on warm serving plates.

5 Carefully lift the salmon steaks from the wok and place on top of the vegetables. Heat the sesame oil and remaining groundnut oil until very hot. Add the asparagus tips and stir-fry for 20 seconds until barely cooked. Season with coarsely ground black pepper. Arrange the tips on top of the fish and pour the hot oil over the top. Serve immediately with rice.

70

Stir-fried Salmon with Leeks

SERVES 4

450 g/1 lb salmon fillet, skinned

2 tbsp kecap manis
    (sweet soy sauce)

2 tbsp tomato ketchup

1 tsp rice vinegar

1 tbsp demerara sugar

1 garlic clove, crushed

4 tbsp groundnut or vegetable oil

450 g/1 lb leeks, thinly shredded

sliced fresh red chillies, to garnish

Method

1 Using a sharp knife, cut the salmon into slices. Place the slices of salmon in a shallow non-metallic dish.

2 Mix the kecap manis, tomato ketchup, vinegar, sugar and garlic together in a small bowl. Pour the mixture over the salmon, toss well and leave to marinate for about 30 minutes.

3 Meanwhile, heat a wok over a medium–high heat, then add 3 tablespoons of the oil. Add the leeks to the wok and stir-fry for about 10 minutes, or until the leeks become crispy and tender.

4 Using a slotted spoon, carefully remove the leeks from the wok and transfer to warmed serving plates.

5 Add the remaining oil to the wok. Add the salmon and the marinade to the wok and cook for 2 minutes. Remove the salmon from the wok, spoon over the leeks, garnish with chillies and serve immediately.

71

Teriyaki Tuna with Vegetables

SERVES 4

4 tuna steaks, about
115 g/4 oz each, cut into strips

225 g/8 oz dried medium
egg noodles

1 tbsp toasted sesame seeds and
2 spring onions, diagonally sliced,
to garnish

Marinade

125 ml/4 fl oz teriyaki sauce

2 tsp clear honey

salt and pepper

Stir-fry

1 tbsp vegetable oil

2 tsp sesame oil

1 carrot, cut into thin strips

2 heads of pak choi, stalks and
leaves separated and finely sliced

1 yellow pepper, deseeded and cut
into thin strips

2 garlic cloves, chopped

1 tbsp soy sauce

Method

1 For the marinade, mix together the teriyaki sauce, honey, and salt and pepper to taste in a shallow dish. Add the tuna and turn to coat in the marinade. Cover with clingfilm and leave to marinate in the refrigerator for 1 hour, turning the tuna occasionally.

2 Cook the noodles according to the packet instructions, until tender. Drain well and set aside.

3 Meanwhile, preheat the grill to high. Line the grill pan with aluminium foil. Remove the tuna from the marinade, reserving the marinade, and arrange in the grill pan. Spoon over half the marinade and cook under the preheated grill for 1 minute. Turn over, spoon over the remaining marinade and cook for a further minute.

4 Heat a wok over a high heat, then add the oils. Stir-fry the carrot, pak choi stalks and yellow pepper for 2 minutes. Add the garlic and pak choi leaves and stir-fry for 1 minute. Add the soy sauce and a little water. Divide the noodles among four individual serving bowls. Top with the stir-fried vegetables, tuna and any cooking juices, and garnish with the sesame seeds and spring onions.

72

Seafood Chow Mein

SERVES 4

85 g/3 oz squid, cleaned

3–4 fresh scallops

85 g/3 oz raw prawns,
   peeled and deveined

1/2 egg white, lightly beaten

2 tsp cornflour, mixed to a paste
   with 21/2 tsp water

275 g/93/4 oz dried fine egg noodles

5–6 tbsp vegetable oil

2 tbsp light soy sauce

55 g/2 oz mangetout,
   sliced diagonally

1/2 tsp salt

1/2 tsp sugar

1 tsp Chinese rice wine

2 spring onions, finely shredded

a few drops of sesame oil

Method

1 Open up the squid and score the inside in a criss-cross pattern, then cut into pieces about 2.5 cm/1 inch square. Soak the squid in a bowl of boiling water until all the pieces curl up. Rinse in cold water and drain.

2 Cut each scallop into 3–4 slices. Cut the prawns in half lengthways if large. Mix the scallops and prawns with the egg white and cornflour.

3 Cook the noodles according to the instructions on the packet, then drain and rinse under cold water. Drain well, then toss with about 1 tablespoon of the oil.

4 Heat 3 tablespoons of the oil in a preheated wok. Add the noodles and 1 tablespoon of the soy sauce and stir-fry for 2–3 minutes. Remove to a large serving dish.

5 Heat the remaining oil in the wok and add the mangetout and seafood. Stir-fry for about 2 minutes, then add the salt, sugar, rice wine, the remaining soy sauce and about half the spring onions. Blend well and add a little water if necessary. Pour the seafood mixture on top of the noodles and sprinkle with sesame oil. Garnish with the remaining spring onions and serve immediately.

73

Seafood Curry

SERVES 4

1 tbsp vegetable oil or
  groundnut oil

3 shallots, finely chopped

2.5-cm/1-inch piece fresh galangal,
  peeled and thinly sliced

2 garlic cloves, finely chopped

400 ml/14 fl oz coconut milk

2 lemon grass stalks,
  snapped in half

4 tbsp fish sauce

2 tbsp chilli sauce

225 g/8 oz raw tiger prawns,
  peeled and deveined

225 g/8 oz baby squid,
  cleaned and thickly sliced

225 g/8 oz salmon fillet,
  skinned and cut into chunks

175 g/6 oz tuna steak,
  cut into chunks

225 g/8 oz fresh mussels,
  scrubbed and debearded

lime wedges, to garnish

cooked jasmine rice, to serve

Method

1 Heat a wok over a medium–high heat, then add the oil. Add the shallots, galangal and garlic and stir-fry for about 2 minutes until they start to soften. Add the coconut milk, lemon grass, fish sauce and chilli sauce. Bring to the boil, reduce the heat and simmer for 1–2 minutes.

2 Add the prawns, squid, salmon and tuna and simmer for 3–4 minutes until the prawns have turned pink and the fish is cooked.

3 Discard any mussels with broken shells or any that refuse to close when tapped. Add the remaining mussels to the wok and cover with a lid. Simmer for 1–2 minutes until they have opened. Discard any mussels that remain closed. Garnish with lime wedges and serve immediately with rice.

74

Quick Seafood Rice

SERVES 4

2 tbsp groundnut or vegetable oil

1 large onion, chopped

1 garlic clove, finely chopped

8 large tomatoes, peeled, deseeded and chopped

225 g/8 oz paella or risotto rice

about 850 ml/1½ pints fish stock

450 g/1 lb mussels, scrubbed and debearded

400 g/14 oz frozen mixed seafood, thawed

175 g/6 oz petit pois, thawed if frozen

2 tbsp chopped fresh parsley, plus extra to garnish

salt and pepper

Method

1 Heat a wok over a high heat, then add the oil. Add the onion and fry until just softened. Add the garlic and half the tomatoes and stir together well. Add the rice and stir-fry for 2–3 minutes, then add half the stock and bring to the boil. Simmer for 12–15 minutes, adding more stock as necessary.

2 Discard any mussels with broken shells and any that refuse to close when tapped. Add the remaining mussels to the wok with the mixed seafood and petit pois. Season to taste with salt and pepper and cook for a further 3–4 minutes, until hot, the mussels have opened and the liquid has been mostly absorbed. Discard any mussels that remain closed.

3 Stir in the remaining tomatoes and the parsley. Taste and adjust the seasoning, adding salt and pepper if needed. Serve immediately, garnished with extra parsley.

75

Teriyaki Prawns

SERVES 4

1½ tbsp groundnut oil

150 g/5½ oz mangetout

150 g/5½ oz baby sweetcorn

1 large orange or yellow pepper,
    deseeded and thinly sliced

8 spring onions, halved lengthways

2 garlic cloves, well crushed

2-cm/¾-inch piece fresh ginger,
    peeled and finely chopped

2 tbsp teriyaki marinade

100 g/3½ oz cashew nuts

400 g/14 oz large cooked
    peeled prawns

1 tbsp sesame oil

Method

1 Heat the groundnut oil in a large, non-stick preheated wok or frying pan, add all the vegetables and stir-fry over a high heat for 4 minutes, or until almost tender. Add the garlic and ginger and stir-fry for 1 minute.

2 Add the teriyaki marinade, cashew nuts and prawns and stir-fry for 2 minutes.

3 Serve immediately, with the sesame oil drizzled over.

76

Prawn Noodle Bowl

SERVES 4

1 bunch spring onions

2 celery sticks

1 red pepper

200 g/7 oz vermicelli rice noodles

2 tbsp groundnut oil

55 g/2 oz unsalted peanuts

1 fresh bird's eye chilli, sliced

1 lemon grass stem, crushed

400 ml/14 fl oz fish stock
   or chicken stock

200 ml/7 fl oz coconut milk

2 tsp Thai fish sauce

350 g/12 oz cooked peeled
   tiger prawns

salt and pepper

3 tbsp chopped fresh coriander,
   to garnish

Method

1 Trim the spring onions and celery and thinly slice diagonally. Deseed and thinly slice the red pepper.

2 Place the noodles in a bowl, cover with boiling water and leave to stand for 4 minutes, or until tender. Drain. Heat the oil in a wok, add the peanuts and stir-fry for 1–2 minutes until golden. Lift out with a slotted spoon. Add the sliced vegetables to the wok and stir-fry over a high heat for 1–2 minutes. Add the chilli, lemon grass, stock, coconut milk and fish sauce and bring to the boil.

3 Stir in the prawns and bring back to the boil, stirring. Season to taste with salt and pepper, then add the noodles. Serve in warmed bowls, sprinkled with fresh coriander.

77

Sesame Noodles with Prawns

SERVES 2

1 tbsp oil

16 raw prawns, peeled and deveined

3 shiitake mushrooms, finely sliced

1/4 white or green cabbage, shredded

1 carrot, grated

2 bundles of somen noodles

6 shiso leaves, shredded

Dressing

3 tbsp oil

1 tbsp sesame seeds, toasted

1/2 cup Japanese rice vinegar

1 tbsp sugar

1 tbsp usukuchi shoyu
   (Japanese light soy sauce)

salt, to taste

Method

1 To make the dressing, mix and all the ingredients together in a non-metallic bowl.

2 Heat the oil in a wok. Add the prawns and cook until pink.

3 Add the mushrooms and stir-fry for 1 minute, then add the cabbage and carrot. Remove from the heat and leave to cool.

4 Cook the noodles according to the packet instructions, then drain.

5 Put the noodles in a bowl and add the prawn mixture, add the dressing and mix well.

6 Sprinkle with the shiso leaves and serve.

78

Scallop Stir-fry

SERVES 4

1 tsp groundnut or vegetable oil

5-cm/2-inch piece fresh ginger, grated

1 tbsp finely grated lime rind

1 orange pepper, deseeded and sliced

1 red onion, thinly sliced

300 g/10½ oz scallops

115 g/4 oz wild mushrooms, such as chanterelle or chestnut mushrooms

50 ml/2 fl oz lime juice

1 tsp clear honey (optional)

1 tbsp soy sauce

115 g/4 oz pak choi, shredded

Method

1 Heat a wok over a high heat, then add the oil. Add the ginger and cook, stirring, for 1 minute.

2 Add the lime rind, pepper and onion and stir-fry for 3–4 minutes, or until the onion has softened. Add the scallops and mushrooms to the wok and stir-fry for 2 minutes.

3 Pour in the lime juice, add the honey, if using, and the soy sauce. Stir together, then add the pak choi and continue to cook for 2–3 minutes, or until the scallops are tender. Serve immediately.

79

Scallop & Mangetout Stir-fry

SERVES 4

3 tbsp groundnut oil

2 tbsp sesame oil

16 large scallops, halved

225 g/8 oz small shiitake
 mushrooms, tough stalks removed

175 g/6 oz mangetout, trimmed and
 halved diagonally

2 tsp finely chopped fresh ginger

2 garlic cloves, finely chopped

2 tsp light soy sauce

juice of 1 lime

3 tbsp torn coriander leaves

salt and pepper

Method

1 Heat a wok over a high heat and add the oils. Stir-fry the scallops for 1 minute. Add the mushrooms and mangetout, and stir-fry for a further minute.

2 Add the ginger, garlic and soy sauce, and a splash of water to moisten. Stir-fry for another 1–2 minutes until the vegetables are just tender.

3 Add the lime juice and coriander leaves, and season to taste with salt and pepper. Divide between plates and serve immediately.

80

Stir-fried Crab with Ginger

SERVES 4

3 tbsp groundnut or vegetable oil

2 large fresh crabs, cleaned, broken into pieces and legs cracked with a cleaver

55 g/2 oz fresh ginger, cut into julienne strips

100 g/3½ oz spring onions, chopped into 5-cm/2-inch lengths

2 tbsp light soy sauce

1 tsp sugar

pinch of white pepper

Method

1 Heat a wok over a high heat, then add 2 tablespoons of the oil. Stir-fry the crab for 3–4 minutes. Remove from the wok and set aside.

2 Heat the remaining oil in the wok, add the ginger and stir until fragrant. Add the spring onions, then stir in the crab pieces. Add the soy sauce, sugar and pepper. Cover and simmer for 1 minute. Serve immediately.

81

Clams in Black Bean Sauce

SERVES 4

900 g/2 lb small clams

1 tbsp vegetable or groundnut oil

1 tsp finely chopped fresh ginger

1 tsp finely chopped garlic

*1 tbsp fermented black beans,
   rinsed and roughly chopped*

2 tsp Chinese rice wine

1 tbsp finely chopped spring onion

1 tsp salt (optional)

Method

1 Discard any clams with broken shells and any that refuse to close when tapped. Wash the remaining clams thoroughly and leave to soak in clean water until ready to cook.

2 In a preheated wok or large frying pan, heat the oil and stir-fry the ginger and garlic until fragrant. Add the black beans and cook for 1 minute.

3 Over a high heat, add the clams and rice wine and stir-fry for 2 minutes to mix everything together. Cover and cook for a further 3 minutes. Add the spring onion and salt, if necessary, and serve immediately.

82

Squid with Black Bean Sauce

SERVES 4

750 g/1 lb 10 oz squid, cleaned and
tentacles discarded

1 large red pepper, deseeded

115 g/4 oz mangetout

1 head of pak choi

1½ tbsp corn oil

1 small fresh red bird's-eye chilli,
chopped

1 garlic clove, finely chopped

1 tsp grated fresh ginger

2 spring onions, chopped

Sauce

3 tbsp black bean sauce

1 tbsp Thai fish sauce

1 tbsp rice wine or dry sherry

1 tbsp dark soy sauce

1 tsp brown sugar

1 tsp cornflour

1 tbsp water

Method

1 Cut the squid body cavities into quarters lengthways. Use the tip of a small, sharp knife to score a diamond pattern into the flesh without cutting all the way through. Pat dry with kitchen paper.

2 Cut the pepper into long, thin slices. Cut the mangetout in half diagonally. Coarsely shred the pak choi.

3 To make the sauce, mix the black bean sauce, fish sauce, rice wine, soy sauce and sugar together in a bowl. Blend the cornflour with the water and stir into the other ingredients in the bowl. Reserve the mixture until required.

4 Heat the oil in a preheated wok. Add the chilli, garlic, ginger and spring onions and stir-fry for 1 minute. Add the pepper slices and stir-fry for 2 minutes.

5 Add the squid and stir-fry over a high heat for a further 1 minute. Stir in the mangetout and pak choi and stir for a further 1 minute or until wilted.

6 Stir in the sauce and cook, stirring constantly, for 2 minutes or until the sauce thickens and clears. Serve immediately.

VEGETABLES

83

Red Curry with Mixed Leaves

SERVES 4

2 tbsp groundnut or vegetable oil

2 onions, thinly sliced

bunch of fine asparagus spears

400 ml/14 fl oz canned coconut milk

2 tbsp Thai red curry paste

3 fresh kaffir lime leaves

225 g/8 oz baby spinach leaves,
   coarse stalks removed

2 heads of pak choi, chopped

1 small head of Chinese leaves,
   shredded

handful of fresh coriander, chopped

cooked rice, to serve

Method

1 Heat a wok over a medium–high heat, then add the oil. Add the onions and asparagus and stir-fry for 1–2 minutes.

2 Add the coconut milk, curry paste and lime leaves and bring gently to the boil, stirring occasionally. Add the spinach, pak choi and Chinese leaves and cook, stirring, for 2–3 minutes, until wilted. Add the coriander and stir well. Serve immediately with rice.

84

Mixed Vegetables with Basil

SERVES 4

2 tbsp vegetable oil or groundnut oil,
plus extra for shallow frying

2 garlic cloves, chopped

1 onion, sliced

115 g/4 oz baby corn, cut in half
diagonally

1/2 cucumber, peeled, halved,
deseeded and sliced

225 g/8 oz canned water chestnuts,
drained and rinsed

55 g/2 oz mangetout

115 g/4 oz shiitake mushrooms,
halved

1 red pepper, deseeded and
thinly sliced

1 tbsp soft light brown sugar

2 tbsp Thai soy sauce

1 tbsp Thai fish sauce

1 tbsp rice vinegar

8–12 sprigs fresh Thai basil

freshly cooked plain rice, to serve

Method

1 Heat a wok over a high heat, then add the oil. Add the garlic and onion and stir-fry for 1–2 minutes. Add the baby corn, cucumber, water chestnuts, mangetout, mushrooms and red pepper and stir-fry for 2–3 minutes, until starting to soften.

2 Add the sugar, soy sauce, fish sauce and vinegar and gradually bring to the boil. Simmer for 1–2 minutes.

3 Meanwhile, heat enough oil for shallow frying in a wok and, when hot, add the basil sprigs. Cook for 20–30 seconds until crisp. Remove with a slotted spoon and drain on kitchen paper.

4 Garnish the vegetable stir-fry with the crispy basil and serve immediately with rice.

85

Hot & Sour Courgettes

SERVES 4

2 large courgettes, thinly sliced

1 tsp salt

2 tbsp groundnut oil

1 tsp Szechuan pepper, crushed

1/2 –1 red chilli, deseeded and sliced
into thin strips

1 large garlic clove, thinly sliced

1/2 tsp finely chopped fresh ginger

1 tbsp rice vinegar

1 tbsp light soy sauce

2 tsp sugar

1 spring onion, green part included,
thinly sliced

a few drops of sesame oil and 1 tsp
sesame seeds, to garnish

Method

1 Put the courgette slices in a large colander and toss with the salt. Cover with a plate and put a weight on top. Leave to drain for 20 minutes. Rinse off the salt and spread out the slices on kitchen paper to dry.

2 Heat a wok over a high heat and add the groundnut oil. Add the Szechuan pepper, chilli, garlic and ginger. Fry for about 20 seconds until the garlic is just beginning to colour.

3 Add the courgette slices and toss in the oil. Add the rice vinegar, soy sauce and sugar, and stir-fry for 2 minutes. Add the spring onion and fry for 30 seconds. Sprinkle with the sesame oil and seeds, and serve immediately.

86

Aubergine Stir-fry

SERVES 4

2 aubergines, peeled

6 tbsp groundnut or vegetable oil

2 red peppers, deseeded and cut into
thin strips

100 g/3½ oz canned water
chestnuts, drained and sliced

6 spring onions, sliced

2 tsp finely chopped fresh ginger

1 large garlic clove, thinly sliced

1 fresh green chilli, deseeded and
finely chopped

150 ml/5 fl oz hot vegetable stock

sesame seeds and thinly sliced spring
onions, to garnish

Sauce

1½ tbsp soy sauce

1½ tbsp rice vinegar

2 tsp sugar

2 tsp cornflour, blended to a smooth
paste with a little water

Method

1 For the sauce, combine the soy sauce, vinegar and sugar in a small bowl, stirring to dissolve the sugar. Mix in the cornflour paste and stir until smooth.

2 Slice the aubergines in half lengthways. With the flat side facing down, slice each half lengthways into 1-cm/½-inch strips. Slice the wider strips lengthways in half again, then cut all the strips crossways into 4-cm/1½-inch pieces.

3 Heat a wok over a high heat, then add 5 tablespoons of the oil. Add the aubergine and red peppers and stir-fry for 2–3 minutes, until just beginning to colour. Remove from the wok and drain on kitchen paper.

4 Heat the remaining tablespoon of oil in the wok over a high heat. Stir-fry the water chestnuts, spring onions, ginger, garlic and chilli for 1 minute.

5 Return the aubergine and red pepper to the wok. Reduce the heat to medium and add the sauce and stock. Stir-fry for 2–3 minutes, until slightly thickened. Sprinkle with sesame seeds and spring onions and serve immediately.

87

Stir-fried Butternut Squash

SERVES 2

1 butternut squash, weighing
about 500 g/1 lb 2 oz

6 large shiitake mushrooms

5 tbsp rapeseed oil

1/2 tsp white peppercorns, crushed

1/2 tsp coriander seeds, crushed

sea salt flakes

2 large garlic cloves, thinly sliced

finely grated zest of 1/2 lemon

1/2 tbsp rice vinegar

4 tbsp chicken or vegetable stock

2 good handfuls of baby spinach,
stalks removed

chopped fresh coriander, to garnish

Method

1 Cut the squash in two between the neck and the rounded part. Remove the skin from each piece. Quarter the rounded part and remove the seeds and fibres. Slice lengthways into thin segments. Slice the neck in half lengthways, then crossways into thin semicircles.

2 Remove and discard the tough stalks from the mushrooms, and thinly slice the caps.

3 Heat a wok over a medium–high heat, then add the oil. Add half the crushed peppercorns and coriander seeds. Stir for a few seconds, then add the squash in small batches. Fry for 5–7 minutes, carefully turning with tongs, until lightly browned and just tender. Sprinkle with sea salt flakes. Using a slotted spoon, transfer to a large sieve set over a bowl.

4 Add the mushrooms to the wok and fry for 4–5 minutes, using some of the oil drained from the squash. Add the garlic and lemon zest, and fry for another minute. Sprinkle with sea salt flakes and the rest of the coriander seeds and peppercorns. Add to the squash.

5 Pour any oil drained from the vegetables into the wok. Stir in the vinegar and stock, and simmer for a few seconds until slightly reduced.

6 Arrange the spinach on individual serving plates. Pile the vegetables on top, then pour over the juices from the wok. Sprinkle with coriander and serve at once.

88

Mushrooms & French Beans

SERVES 2

450 g/1 lb mixed small mushrooms
  such as cremini, enoki and
  buna shimeji

6 tbsp rapeseed oil

1 tsp coriander seeds, crushed

1 fresh bay leaf

175 g/6 oz French beans

1 large garlic clove, thinly sliced

3 tbsp lemon juice

2 tsp soy sauce

2 tbsp chopped coriander

2 tsp sesame oil

2 tsp sesame seeds

salt and pepper

Method

1 Rinse the mushrooms and dry with kitchen paper. If using clumping mushrooms, such as enoki and buna shimeji, slice off the root and separate the clump. Slice cremini mushrooms in half.

2 Heat a wok over a medium–high heat and add the oil. Add the coriander seeds and bay leaf, and fry for a few seconds to flavour the oil. Add the mushrooms and beans, and stir-fry for 5 minutes.

3 Stir in the garlic, lemon juice and soy sauce. Season with salt and pepper, and stir-fry for 2 minutes. Sprinkle with the coriander, sesame oil and seeds, and fry for a few seconds. Serve hot, warm or at room temperature.

89

Oyster Mushrooms & Vegetable

SERVES 4

1 tbsp vegetable or groundnut oil

4 spring onions, finely sliced

1 carrot, cut into thin strips

1 courgette, cut into thin strips

1/2 head of broccoli, cut into florets

450 g/1 lb oyster mushrooms, thinly sliced

2 tbsp crunchy peanut butter

1 tsp chilli powder, or to taste

3 tbsp water

lime wedges, to garnish

freshly cooked rice, to serve

Method

1 Heat the oil in a preheated wok or large frying pan until almost smoking. Stir-fry the spring onions for 1 minute. Add the carrot and courgette and stir-fry for another minute. Then add the broccoli and cook for one more minute.

2 Stir in the mushrooms and cook until they are soft and at least half the liquid they produce has evaporated. Add the peanut butter and stir well, then season with the chilli powder to taste. Finally add the water and cook for 1 minute.

3 Garnish with lime wedges and serve with freshly cooked rice.

90

Vegetable Stir-fry

SERVES 4

2 tbsp groundnut oil or vegetable oil

1 bunch of spring onions,
   roughly chopped

2.5-cm/1-inch piece fresh ginger,
   finely chopped

2 lemon grass stalks, halved

2 carrots, peeled and
   cut into matchsticks

1 small head of broccoli,
   cut into florets

55 g/2 oz baby corn, halved
   lengthways

55 g/2 oz canned water chestnuts,
   drained

1 tbsp red curry paste

225 g/8 oz dried medium
   egg noodles

4 tbsp sesame seeds

salt

Method

1 Heat the oil in a preheated wok, add the spring onions,
ginger and lemon grass and stir-fry over a medium–high heat for
2–3 minutes, until starting to soften. Add the carrots, broccoli and
baby corn and stir-fry for 3–4 minutes, until starting to soften. Add
the water chestnuts and curry paste and stir well, then stir-fry for a
further 2–3 minutes. Discard the lemon grass.

2 Meanwhile, bring a large saucepan of lightly salted water to the
boil, add the noodles and cook for 4–5 minutes, or until just tender.
Drain and return to the saucepan. Add the sesame seeds and toss
to coat.

3 Add the noodles to the stir-fried vegetables and serve
immediately.

91

Carrot & Pumpkin Curry

SERVES 4

150 ml/5 fl oz vegetable stock

2.5-cm/1-inch piece fresh galangal, sliced

2 garlic cloves, chopped

1 lemon grass stalk (white part only), finely chopped

2 fresh red chillies, deseeded and chopped

4 carrots, cut into chunks

225 g/8 oz pumpkin, deseeded and cut into cubes

2 tbsp vegetable or groundnut oil

2 shallots, finely chopped

3 tbsp Thai yellow curry paste

400 ml/14 fl oz coconut milk

4–6 sprigs of fresh Thai basil

25 g/1 oz toasted pumpkin seeds, to garnish

Method

1 Pour the stock into a large saucepan and bring to the boil. Add the galangal, half the garlic, the lemon grass and chillies and simmer for 5 minutes. Add the carrots and pumpkin and simmer for 5–6 minutes, until tender.

2 Meanwhile, heat the oil in a wok or frying pan and stir-fry the shallots and the remaining garlic for 2–3 minutes. Add the curry paste and stir-fry for 1–2 minutes.

3 Stir the shallot mixture into the saucepan and add the coconut milk and Thai basil. Simmer for 2–3 minutes. Serve hot, sprinkled with the toasted pumpkin seeds.

92

Tofu & Vegetable Curry

SERVES 4

vegetable or groundnut oil,
   for deep-frying

225 g/8 oz firm tofu, drained and cut
   into cubes

2 tbsp vegetable or groundnut oil

2 onions, chopped

2 garlic cloves, chopped

1 fresh red chilli, deseeded and sliced

3 celery sticks, diagonally sliced

225 g/8 oz mushrooms, thickly sliced

115 g/4 oz baby corn, cut in half

1 red pepper, deseeded and
   cut into strips

3 tbsp Thai red curry paste

400 ml/14 fl oz coconut milk

1 tsp palm sugar or soft,
   light brown sugar

2 tbsp Thai soy sauce

225 g/8 oz baby spinach leaves

Method

1 Heat the oil for deep-frying in a preheated wok or a deep saucepan to 180–190°C/350–375°F, or until a cube of bread browns in 30 seconds. Add the tofu cubes, in batches, and cook for 4–5 minutes until crisp and brown all over. Remove with a slotted spoon and drain on kitchen paper.

2 Heat the 2 tablespoons of oil in a wok or frying pan and stir-fry the onions, garlic and chilli for 1–2 minutes, until they start to soften. Add the celery, mushrooms, corn cobs and red pepper and stir-fry for 3–4 minutes, until they soften.

3 Stir in the curry paste and coconut milk and gradually bring to the boil. Add the sugar and soy sauce and then the spinach. Cook, stirring constantly, until the spinach has wilted. Serve immediately, topped with the tofu.

93

Mangetout & Tofu Stir-fry

SERVES 2–3

2 tbsp sesame oil

3 tbsp groundnut oil

200 g/7 oz small shiitake
   mushrooms

2 heads of pak choi, leaves left
   whole, stalks sliced

150 g/5½ oz mangetout,
   diagonally halved

250 g/9 oz firm tofu, drained and
   cut into cubes

3-cm/1¼-inch piece fresh ginger,
   thinly sliced

2 garlic cloves, finely chopped

1 tbsp soy sauce

1 tsp sesame seeds

salt and pepper

cooked noodles, to serve

Method

1 Heat a wok with a lid over a medium–high heat, then add
the oils. Add the mushrooms, pak choi stalks and mangetout,
and stir-fry for 1 minute.

2 Add the tofu, pak choi leaves, ginger, garlic and a splash of
water to moisten. Stir-fry for a further 1–2 minutes, until the
pak choi leaves have wilted.

3 Stir in the soy sauce, sprinkle with the sesame seeds
and season to taste with salt and pepper. Serve immediately
with noodles.

94

Spicy Tofu

SERVES 4

250 g/9 oz firm tofu, drained and cut
into cubes

4 tbsp groundnut oil

1 tbsp grated fresh ginger

3 garlic cloves, crushed

4 spring onions, thinly sliced

1 head of broccoli, cut into florets

1 carrot, cut into thin strips

1 yellow pepper, deseeded and thinly
sliced

250 g/9 oz shiitake mushrooms,
thinly sliced

steamed rice, to serve

Marinade

75 ml/2½ fl oz vegetable stock

2 tsp cornflour

2 tbsp soy sauce

1 tbsp caster sugar

pinch of chilli flakes

Method

1 To make the marinade, blend the vegetable stock, cornflour, soy sauce, sugar and chilli flakes together in a large bowl. Add the tofu and toss well to cover in the marinade. Set aside to marinate for 20 minutes.

2 In a large wok, heat 2 tablespoons of the groundnut oil and stir-fry the tofu with its marinade until brown and crispy. Remove from the wok and set aside.

3 Heat the remaining 2 tablespoons of groundnut oil in the wok and stir-fry the ginger, garlic and spring onions for 30 seconds. Add the broccoli, carrot, yellow pepper and mushrooms to the wok and cook for 5–6 minutes. Return the tofu to the wok and stir-fry to reheat. Serve immediately over freshly steamed rice.

95

Tofu Laksa with Noodles

SERVES 4

850 ml/1 1/2 pints vegetable stock

400 ml/14 fl oz coconut milk

250 g/9 oz shiitake mushrooms, stalks removed, thinly sliced

150 g/5 1/2 oz firm tofu, drained and cut into cubes

2 tbsp tomato purée

175 g/6 oz fine egg noodles

salt and pepper

8 spring onions, sliced, and 4 tbsp shredded mint leaves, to garnish

lime wedges, to serve

Spice paste

2 red chillies, deseeded and chopped

4-cm/1 1/2-inch piece fresh ginger, chopped

2 large garlic cloves, chopped

2 lemon grass stalks, tough outer layers removed, inner stalks chopped

1 tsp coriander seeds, crushed

6 macadamia nuts, chopped

small handful of coriander leaves

3 tbsp vegetable oil

Method

1 Purée the spice paste ingredients in a food processor, pulsing several times until smooth.

2 Heat a wok over a medium–high heat, add the spice paste and stir-fry for 30 seconds. Pour in the stock and coconut milk, and bring to the boil. Add the mushrooms, tofu and tomato purée and season with salt and pepper. Simmer gently for 5 minutes.

3 Bring a large saucepan of lightly salted water to the boil, add the noodles and cook for 4 minutes, or according to the instructions on the packet, until soft. Divide between four large warmed soup bowls. Ladle the spicy broth over the noodles. Garnish with sliced spring onions and shredded mint leaves and serve with lime wedges.

96

Crispy Noodle Stir-fry

SERVES 4

peanut or sunflower oil,
  for deep-frying

115 g/4 oz rice vermicelli, broken
  into 7.5-cm/3-inch lengths

115 g/4 oz French beans,
  cut into short lengths

2 carrots, cut into thin sticks

2 courgettes, cut into thin sticks

115 g/4 oz shiitake mushrooms,
  sliced

2.5-cm/1-inch piece fresh ginger,
  shredded

1/2 small head Napa cabbage,
  shredded

4 spring onions, shredded

85 g/3 oz fresh beansprouts

2 tbsp dark soy sauce

2 tbsp Chinese rice wine

large pinch of sugar

2 tbsp roughly chopped
  fresh coriander

Method

1 Heat a large wok over a high heat. Pour in the oil and heat to 180°C/350°F or until a cube of bread browns in 30 seconds. Add the noodles, in batches, and cook for 1 1/2–2 minutes, or until crisp and puffed up. Remove and drain on kitchen paper. Pour off all but 2 tablespoons of oil from the wok.

2 Heat the remaining oil over high heat. Add the French beans and stir-fry for 2 minutes. Add the carrot and courgette sticks, sliced mushrooms and ginger and stir-fry for a further 2 minutes.

3 Add the shredded Napa cabbage, spring onions and beansprouts and stir-fry for a further minute. Add the soy sauce, rice wine and sugar and cook, stirring constantly, for 1 minute.

4 Add the chopped coriander and toss well. Serve immediately, with the noodles.

97

Noodles with Tofu & Mushroom:

SERVES 4

3 tbsp groundnut oil

2 dried red chillies

250 g/9 oz medium egg noodles

1 garlic clove, crushed

200 g/7 oz firm tofu, drained and
cut into 1-cm/½-inch cubes

200 g/7 oz oyster or chestnut
mushrooms, sliced

2 tbsp lime juice

2 tbsp soy sauce

1 tsp brown sugar

fresh red chillies, to garnish

Method

1 Heat the oil in a wok and add the chillies. Heat gently for 10 minutes. Discard the fried chillies.

2 Cook the noodles in boiling water for 4 minutes, or according to the packet instructions. Drain.

3 Add the garlic and tofu to the wok and stir-fry on a high heat until golden. Remove with a slotted spoon and keep hot.

4 Add the mushrooms to the wok and stir-fry for 2–3 minutes to soften.

5 Stir in the lime juice, soy sauce and sugar.

6 Return the noodles and tofu to the wok and toss to mix thoroughly.

7 Serve immediately, garnished with fresh chillies.

98

Noodle Stir-fry

SERVES 2

140 g/5 oz dried wide rice noodles

6 tbsp soy sauce

2 tbsp lemon juice

1 tsp granulated sugar

1/2 tsp cornflour

1 tbsp groundnut or vegetable oil

2 tsp grated fresh ginger

2 garlic cloves, chopped

4–5 spring onions, sliced

2 tbsp Chinese rice wine
    or dry sherry

200 g/7 oz canned water chestnuts,
    drained and sliced

Method
1 Put the noodles in a large bowl, cover with boiling water and soak for 4 minutes, or cook according to the packet instructions, until tender. Drain and rinse under cold running water.
2 Combine the soy sauce, lemon juice, sugar and cornflour in a small bowl.
3 Heat a wok over a medium–high heat, then add the oil. Add the ginger and garlic and stir-fry for 1 minute. Add the spring onions and stir-fry for 3 minutes.
4 Add the rice wine, followed by the soy sauce mixture and cook for 1 minute.
5 Stir in the water chestnuts and noodles and cook for a further 1–2 minutes, or until heated through. Serve immediately.

99

Egg-fried Rice

SERVES 4

2 tbsp vegetable or groundnut oil

350 g/12 oz cooked rice, chilled

1 egg, well beaten

Method

1 Heat the oil in a preheated wok and stir-fry the rice for 1 minute, breaking it down as much as possible into individual grains.

2 Quickly add the egg, stirring, so as to coat each piece of rice. Stir until the egg is cooked and the rice, as far as possible, is in single grains. Serve immediately.

100

Spring Vegetable Rice

SERVES 4

2 tbsp groundnut or vegetable oil

2 shallots, chopped

2 garlic cloves, crushed

225 g/8 oz basmati rice

about 600 ml/1 pint chicken stock

1 tbsp Thai red curry paste

1 tsp Thai fish sauce

3 tbsp soy sauce

175 g/6 oz baby corn,
  halved lengthways

115 g/4 oz baby carrots,
  halved lengthways

55 g/2 oz sugar snap peas

55 g/2 oz fresh beansprouts

4 tbsp sesame seeds

handful of fresh coriander, chopped

2 tbsp sesame oil

salt

Method

1 Heat a wok over a medium–high heat, then add the groundnut oil. Add the shallots and garlic and stir-fry for 1–2 minutes. Add the rice and stir-fry for 2–3 minutes.

2 Add the stock, curry paste, fish sauce and soy sauce and bring to the boil, stirring occasionally. Reduce the heat and simmer for 10–12 minutes, until the rice is tender, adding more stock or boiling water, if necessary.

3 Meanwhile, cook the baby corn and carrots in a saucepan of lightly salted boiling water for 2–3 minutes, until just tender. Add the sugar snap peas and cook for 1 minute. Add the beansprouts and stir well, then drain.

4 Heat a dry frying pan until hot, add the sesame seeds and cook over a medium–high heat, shaking the frying pan frequently, for 30–45 seconds, until lightly browned.

5 Add the drained vegetables, coriander and sesame oil to the rice and mix well. Serve immediately, scattered with the toasted sesame seeds.

Index

crab
  Crab Wontons 22
  Spicy Warm Crab & Prawn Salad 50
  Stir-fried Crab with Ginger 174
Crispy Noodle Stir-fry 208
Crispy Pork Dumplings 12
Crispy 'Seaweed' 26
Crispy Sesame Prawns 20
cucumber
  Cantonese Sweet & Sour Duck 132
  Gado Gado 52
  Mixed Vegetables with Basil 184
curries
  Carrot & Pumpkin Curry 198
  Green Chicken Curry 98
  Red Lamb Curry 82
  Seafood Curry 160
  Thai Green Fish Curry 140
  Tofu & Vegetable Curry 200

duck
  Cantonese Sweet & Sour Duck 132
  Duck with Black Beans 134
  Duck with Mixed Peppers 130
  Three-pea Stir-fry with Duck 136

eggs
  Chicken Fried Rice 118
  Chinese Rice with Egg 16
  Egg-fried Rice 214
  Gado Gado 52
  Pad Noodles with Pork & Prawns 90
  Prawns Fu Yung 150

fish
  Cod with Spiced Noodles 146
  Fish with Tomatoes & Herbs 148
  Fried Fish with Pine Nuts 142
  Rice Noodles with Yellow Fish 144
  Seafood Curry 160
  Steamed Salmon with
    Asparagus 152
  Stir-fried Salmon with Leeks 154

Teriyaki Tuna with Vegetables 156
Thai Green Fish Curry 140
Fried Fish with Pine Nuts 142

Gado Gado 52
garlic
  Hoisin Pork with Garlic Noodles 92
  Pad Noodles with Pork & Prawns 90
  Pork & Cabbage Gyoza 14
ginger
  Chicken with Cashew Nuts 102
  Crab Wontons 22
  Ginger Beef with Yellow Peppers 68
  Ginger Chicken with Noodles 120
  Ginger Pork with Mushrooms 94
  Gingered Chicken Salad 46
  Mushroom & Ginger Soup 40
  Sichuan Peppered Beef 60
  Stir-fried Crab with Ginger 174
  Vegetable Stir-fry 196
Gong Bau Chicken 112
Green Chicken Curry 98
Green Lamb Stir-fry 80

herbs
  Fish with Tomatoes & Herbs 148
Hoisin Pork with Garlic Noodles 92
Hoisin Turkey 126
Honey-glazed Roast Pork 86
Hot & Sour Courgettes 186
Hot & Sour Soup Tom Yum 36
Hot & Sour Vegetable Salad 48
Hot Sesame Beef 64

lamb
  Green Lamb Stir-fry 80
  Lamb with Black Bean Sauce 76
  Red Lamb Curry 82
  Stir-fried Lamb with Orange 78
leeks
  Stir-fried Salmon with Leeks 154
lemon grass
  Hot & Sour Soup Tom Yum 36

Pork with Basil & Lemon Grass 88
Prawn Noodle Bowl 166
Seafood Curry 160
Thai-style Seafood Soup 38
Vegetable Stir-fry 196
Lemon Turkey with Spinach 128

mangetout
  Ginger Beef with Yellow Peppers 68
  Gingered Chicken Salad 46
  Hot & Sour Vegetable Salad 48
  Mangetout & Tofu Stir-fry 202
  Marinated Beef with Vegetables 66
  Peppered Chicken Stir-fry 108
  Scallop & Mangetout Stir-fry 172
  Spicy Warm Crab & Prawn Salad 50
  Three-pea Stir-fry with Duck 136
Marinated Beef with Celery 74
Marinated Beef with Vegetables 66
Mixed Vegetables with Basil 184
mushrooms
  Beef Chop Suey 62
  Beef with Mixed Mushrooms 72
  Chicken Chow Mein 100
  Chicken with Cashew Nuts 102
  Chicken with Pistachio Nuts 114
  Fried Fish with Pine Nuts 142
  Ginger Pork with Mushrooms 94
  Hot & Sour Soup Tom Yum 36
  Mushrooms & French Beans 192
  Mushroom & Ginger Soup 40
  Noodles with Tofu &
    Mushrooms 210
  Oyster Mushrooms &
    Vegetables 194
  Pork with Basil & Lemon Grass 88
  Rainbow Salad 42
  Scallop & Mangetout Stir-fry 172
  Scallop Stir-fry 170
  Spring Rolls 10
  Stir-fried Butternut Squash 190
  Tempura Vegetables 24
  Turkey with Pak Choi 124

mussels
   Quick Seafood Rice 162
   Seafood Curry 160

noodles
   Beef & Noodle Soup 28
   Beef Chow Mein 58
   Chicken Noodle Soup 32
   Chinese Chicken Salad 44
   Cod with Spiced Noodles 146
   Crispy Noodle Stir-fry 208
   Ginger Chicken with Noodles 120
   Gingered Chicken Salad 46
   Green Lamb Stir-fry 80
   Hoisin Pork with Garlic Noodles 92
   Mushroom & Ginger Soup 40
   Noodle Stir-fry 212
   Noodles with Tofu &
     Mushrooms 210
   Pad Noodles with Pork & Prawns 90
   Prawn Noodle Bowl 166
   Rice Noodles with Yellow Fish 144
   Sesame Noodles with Prawns 168
   Teriyaki Tuna with Vegetables 156
   Tofu Laksa with Noodles 206
   Yaki Soba 106

onions
   Hot & Sour Vegetable Salad 48
   Mixed Vegetables with Basil 184
   Sichuan Peppered Beef 60
   Stir-fried Lamb with Orange 78
   Sweet & Sour Chicken 104
   Tempura Vegetables 24
orange
   Stir-fried Lamb with Orange 78
Oyster Mushrooms & Vegetables 194

Pad Noodles with Pork & Prawns 90
pak choi
   Beef & Pak Choi Stir-fry 70
   Hot & Sour Soup Tom Yum 36
   Red Curry with Mixed Leaves 182

Squid with Black Bean Sauce 178
Teriyaki Tuna with Vegetables 156
Turkey with Pak Choi 124
peanuts
   Gong Bau Chicken 112
   Green Lamb Stir-fry 80
   Pad Noodles with Pork & Prawns 90
   Rice Noodles with Yellow Fish 144
peas
   Chicken Fried Rice 118
   Three-Pea Stir fry with Duck 136
peppercorns
   Beef & Noodle Soup 28
   Peppered Chicken Stir-fry 108
   Sichuan Peppered Beef 60
peppers
   Aubergine Stir-fry 188
   Beef Chow Mein 58
   Chicken Chow Mein 100
   Chicken with Cashew Nuts 102
   Crab Wontons 22
   Duck with Mixed Peppers 130
   Fried Fish with Pine Nuts 142
   Ginger Beef with Yellow Peppers 68
   Hot & Sour Vegetable Salad 48
   Hot Sesame Beef 64
   Lamb with Black Bean Sauce 76
   Marinated Beef with Celery 74
   Rainbow Salad 42
   Scallop Stir-fry 170
   Sliced Beef in Black Bean Sauce 56
   Sweet & Sour Spare Ribs 30
   Tempura Vegetables 24
pine nuts
   Fried Fish with Pine Nuts 142
pineapple
   Sweet & Sour Pork 84
   Sweet & Sour Spare Ribs 30
pistachios
   Chicken with Pistachio Nuts 114
pork
   Crispy Pork Dumplings 12
   Ginger Pork with Mushrooms 94
   Hoisin Pork with Garlic Noodles 92

Honey-glazed Roast Pork 86
Pad Noodles with Pork & Prawns 90
Pork & Cabbage Gyoza 14
Pork with Basil & Lemon Grass 88
Spring Rolls 10
Sweet & Sour Pork 84
Sweet & Sour Spare Ribs 30
prawns
   Crispy Sesame Prawns 20
   Pad Noodles with Pork & Prawns 90
   Prawn Noodle Bowl 166
   Prawn Toasts 18
   Prawns Fu Yung 150
   Seafood Chow Mein 158
   Seafood Curry 160
   Sesame Noodles with Prawns 168
   Spicy Warm Crab & Prawn Salad 50
   Spring Rolls 10
   Squid & Prawn Laksa 34
   Teriyaki Prawns 164
   Thai-style seafood soup 38
   Yaki Soba 106
Pumpkin & Carrot Curry 198

Quick Seafood Rice 162

Rainbow Salad 42
Red Curry with Mixed Leaves 182
Red Lamb Curry 82
rice
   Chicken Fried Rice 118
   Chinese Rice with Egg 16
   Egg-fried Rice 214
   Quick Seafood Rice 162
   Spring Vegetable Rice 216
Rice Noodles with Yellow Fish 144

salmon
   Steamed Salmon with
     Asparagus 152
   Stir-fried Salmon with Leeks 154
scallops
   Scallop & Mangetout Stir-fry 172
   Scallop Stir-fry 170

Seafood Chow Mein 158
Thai-style Seafood Soup 38
seafood
Quick Seafood Rice 162
Seafood Chow Mein 158
Seafood Curry 160
Thai-style Seafood Soup 38
sesame
Crispy Sesame Prawns 20
Hot Sesame Beef 64
Sesame Noodles with Prawns 168
shallots
Beef & Noodle Soup 28
Beef & Pak Choi Stir-fry 70
Beef with Mixed Mushrooms 72
Carrot & Pumpkin Curry 198
Chicken Fried Rice 118
Pad Noodles with Pork & Prawns 90
Sichuan Peppered Beef 60
Sliced Beef in Black Bean Sauce 56
Spice Chicken with Courgettes 116
Spicy Tofu 204
Spicy Warm Crab & Prawn Salad 50
spinach
Chinese Rice with Egg 16
Lemon Turkey with Spinach 128
Marinated Beef with Vegetables 66
Red Curry with Mixed Leaves 182
spring onions
Chicken Chow Mein 100
Chicken Noodle Soup 32
Chinese Chicken Salad 44
Green Lamb Stir-fry 80
Lemon Turkey with Spinach 128
Oyster Mushrooms &
   Vegetables 194
Peppered Chicken Stir-fry 108
Rainbow Salad 42
Rice Noodles with Yellow Fish 144
Squid & Prawn Laksa 34
Teriyaki Prawns 164

Turkey Teriyaki 122
Vegetable Stir-fry 196
Spring Rolls 10
Spring Vegetable Rice 216
squid
Seafood Chow Mein 158
Seafood Curry 160
Squid & Prawn Laksa 34
Squid with Black Bean Sauce 178
Steamed Salmon with Asparagus 152
Stir-fried Butternut Squash 190
Stir-fried Crab with Ginger 174
Stir-fried Lamb with Orange 78
Stir-fried Salmon with Leeks 154
Sweet & Sour Chicken 104
Sweet & Sour Pork 84
Sweet & Sour Spare Ribs 30
sweetcorn
Ginger Beef with Yellow Peppers 68
Gingered Chicken Salad 46
Hot & Sour Vegetable Salad 48
Mixed Vegetables with Basil 184
Rainbow Salad 42
Vegetable Stir-fry 196

Tempura Vegetables 24
Teriyaki Chicken 110
Teriyaki Prawns 164
Teriyaki Tuna with Vegetables 156
Teriyaki Turkey 122
Thai Green Fish Curry 140
Thai-style Seafood Soup 38
Three-pea Stir-fry with Duck 136
tofu
Gado Gado 52
Hot & Sour Soup Tom Yum 36
Mangetout & Tofu Stir-fry 202
Spicy Tofu 204
Tofu & Vegetable Curry 200
Tofu Laksa with Noodles 206

tomatoes
Duck with Mixed Peppers 130
Fish with Tomatoes & Herbs 148
Quick Seafood Rice 162
tuna
Teriyaki Tuna with Vegetables 156
turkey
Lemon Turkey with Spinach 128
Turkey Teriyaki 122
Turkey with Hoisin Sauce 126
Turkey with Pak Choi 124

vegetables
Hot & Sour Vegetable Salad 48
Marinated Beef with Vegetables 66
Mixed Vegetables with Basil 184
Oyster Mushrooms &
   Vegetables 194
Spring Vegetable Rice 216
Tempura Vegetables 24
Teriyaki Tuna with Vegetables 156
Tofu & Vegetable Curry 200
Vegetable Stir-fry 196

water chestnuts
Aubergine Stir-fry 188
Beef Chop Suey 62
Chicken with Pistachio Nuts 114
Noodle Stir-fry 212
Peppered Chicken Stir-fry 108
Pork with Basil & Lemon Grass 88
Red Lamb Curry 82
Vegetable Stir-fry 196
wontons
Crab Wontons 22
Crispy Pork Dumplings 12
Pork & Cabbage Gyoza 14

Yaki Soba 106